British Bee-Farming, Its profits and Pleasures

James F. Robinson

Copyright © BiblioLife, LLC

BiblioLife Reproduction Series: Our goal at BiblioLife is to help readers, educators and researchers by bringing back in print hard-to-find original publications at a reasonable price and, at the same time, preserve the legacy of literary history. The following book represents an authentic reproduction of the text as printed by the original publisher and may contain prior copyright references. While we have attempted to accurately maintain the integrity of the original work(s), from time to time there are problems with the original book scan that may result in minor errors in the reproduction, including imperfections such as missing and blurred pages, poor pictures, markings and other reproduction issues beyond our control. Because this work is culturally important, we have made it available as a part of our commitment to protecting, preserving and promoting the world's literature.

All of our books are in the "public domain" and some are derived from Open Source projects dedicated to digitizing historic literature. We believe that when we undertake the difficult task of re-creating them as attractive, readable and affordable books, we further the mutual goal of sharing these works with a larger audience. A portion of BiblioLife profits go back to Open Source projects in the form of a donation to the groups that do this important work around the world. If you would like to make a donation to these worthy Open Source projects, or would just like to get more information about these important initiatives, please visit www.bibliolife.com/opensource.

BRITISH BEE-FARMING

ITS

PROFITS AND PLEASURES.

Dedicated to

MY BROTHER,

THE GENIAL AND KIND-HEARTED VILLAGE DOCTOR,

WHO GAVE ME MY FIRST

STOCK OF BEES.

CONTENTS.

PART I.

Practical Bee-farming.

	PAGE
The System of Bee-farming	5
Bee-farmer's Hive	8
Details and Measurement of the Bee-farmer's Hive	19
Management of Bee-farmer's Hive	22
Thickness of the Hive	24
Hive Entrance	25
British Bee-farmer's Honey-extractor	26
How to use the Extractor	28
When to commence Bee-farming	30
Modern Bee-hives	33
Neighbour's Glass Woodbury Hives	34
Cottage Hives	36
Pettitt's Improved Straw Hive	36
Pettitt's Cottage Hive	38
Narbonne Hive	38
Yates' Round-topped Hive	40
Removing Supers from the Hive	41
How to Manufacture Straw Hives	42
Hive-Bonnets	44
Rustic Bee-sheds	46
Situation of the Apiary	49
The Bee-sting	52
Remedies for the Bee-sting	58
The Swarming Season	63
American Swarm Signal	66
Hiving Swarms in High Trees	68
On Feeding Bees	70
How to prepare Barley-sugar for Bee-feeding	82
Bee-pastures	84
A List of Plants suitable for Bee-culture	89
Pollen, or Bee-bread	92
Propolis, or Hive Cement and Varnish	99
How to avoid the Brimstone-pit	104
How to drive Bees	105
Uniting Stocks	107

viii   *CONTENTS.*

PART II.

INHABITANTS OF THE HIVE.

	PAGE
Notes and Hints about Bees	111
The Queen-bee	113
The Worker-bee	118
Drones	120
Why so many Drones are produced	122
Strange Theories respecting Drones	121
Appearance of Drone-bees	123
Massacre of the Drones	123
How long do Drones live?	124
Queen's Wedding	125
How to regulate or keep down the Drones	126
The Drone-catcher	126
Ligurian, or Italian Bees	128
The Value of Italians	130
How to fill the Apiary with Italian Stocks	132
Bees in other Lands	134
Sagacity of Bees	142
Senses of Bees	143
Foreign Bees	146
Foul-brood	149
The Enemies of our Honey-bee	153
The worst Bee-enemies	164
Superstitious Notions respecting Bees	169
A North American Bee-hunt	174
Australian Bee-hunting	178
The Bee-hunter	179
Golden Rules	187

Bee-Farmer's Calendar :—

Work for January	190
Work for February	191
Work for March	193
Work for April	194
Work for May	197
Work for June	198
Work for July	200
Work for August	201
Work for September	203
Work for October	204
Work for November	205
Work of December	206

LIST OF ILLUSTRATIONS.

	PAGE
Bee-Farmer's Hive	16
Measurement of do.	19
Honey-Extractor (closed)	27
Do. (open)	27
Do. (comb in box)	28
Do. (wire bars)	29
Glass Woodbury Hive	35
Pettitt's Improved Cottage Hive	36
„ Cottage Skep	38
Narbonne Hive	39
Yates' Round-topped Hive	40
Cheshire's Bee-Trap	42
Skep-making	43
Skep Bonnets	45
Rustic Bee-Shed	47
Swarm Signal	67
Mode of securing Swarms	69
Lancashire Bee-Feeder	78
Queen, Drone, and Worker Bees	111
Drone Cage	127
Nest of *Vespa sylvestris*	165

PREFACE.

VERY few words are needed by way of preface to this little work. The author trusts that it will be found to be practical, for it has been his intention throughout to make it so simple that any village bee-keeper may with ease follow its teaching, especially those who may have the happiness to possess a hive of bees in the cottage garden, and delight to listen to their cheery song, when seated after the toils of the day on the rustic bench, shaded with the trailing woodbine. It is better to be practical than scientific; nor has the author aimed at any elegance of style, preferring that the merit of the book should lie in its simplicity and reliability. His principal desire has been to benefit the large and increasingly intelligent class of bee-keepers in this country. It is certain anyone can keep bees without the aid of a guide-book or manual on bee-keeping, but it is equally true that no one in this age of progress can afford to dispense with the experience of those who have spent years in learning what they are again wishful to teach others. The author hopes that, by the perusal of these pages, he may induce many to keep bees who have not hitherto done so; that he may enable those who have done well with the old fashioned system to do much better in future; and that he may persuade all to become bee-farmers in the true acceptation of the term; for those who have kept only two or three stocks may just as easily and with little extra expense keep a hundred. If they will do so, they may rely on a good income from their bee-farm, for we have no hesitation in saying, that, in proportion to the capital expended, bee-farming will be found the most profitable business known.

Let Tennyson's farmer's proverb be learned by heart at the outset,

> "Them as has munny has all. Wots beauty? the flower as blaws.
> But proputty, proputty sticks, an' proputty, proputty graws."

Then gradually increase your stocks by natural swarming, and look well after your bee-farm; it will speedily yield a rich return.

Remember—

> The wise and active conquer difficulties
> By daring to attempt them, Folly and Sloth
> Shiver and shrink at sight of toil and trouble,
> And make the impossibilities they fear.

FRODSHAM,
    May 1880.

PART I.

PRACTICAL BEE-FARMING.

BEE-FARMING.

This is a new name; but any trade which gathers the produce of the soil may be called farming, and the place where it is carried on a farm. The culture of bees, therefore, may well be termed Bee-farming. There are so many books on bees, written for the purpose of palming off some hive upon the public, that bee-keeping has obtained an ill name with many, and has often been given up in despair, being looked upon merely as a hobby suitable only for those who can throw away a few hundred pounds upon it. We hope, however, to dispel these illusions. Our experience is this: Bee-farming, if rightly worked, is really a money-making profession, but to make it profitable we must first throw overboard every hive which is too large to be workable, and then invest a few shillings upon the Italian honey-extractor.

No trade can be profitable unless attention and care are expended upon it. In every trade, if instead of throwing all your energy into it you grow careless or idle, and never look after your business, it cannot succeed. Just so with Bee-farming; look well after your stocks and they will richly reward your efforts. We have no doubt any cottager living in a village, who has fifteen hives, which is but a small number, might derive a far higher income from his bees than from manual labour, if our

BEE-FARMING.

system is adopted. If the hives in the Alps, with very little summer to labour in, can turn out a good honey harvest, what may not an English labourer expect?

To show the yield by good management in the British islands we quote the following from Pettigrew's work:

"Robert Read, of Carluke, states that from one hive, with its swarms, he obtained, in 1864, 328 lbs. as follows:

Mother hive (old stock) . .	92 lbs.
First swarm	160 ,,
Second swarm	76 ,,
Total .	328 lbs."

In 1866 he had a hive of 148 lbs.
In 1869 he *took* 400 lbs. from ten stocks.

Our experience has scarcely given so high a yield of honey as the above, partly because our stocks are kept in the neighbourhood of large chemical works, where vegetation is not nearly so vigorous as in more favoured localities.

We live in a practical age. Proposals of all sorts are weighed against gold. "How much will it bring? Can I turn an honest penny by this business?" We do not pretend to say bee-farmers are rich men, or that the way to a fortune is through a bee-hive, but we do assert that a poor curate, vicar, or cottager working all day on the neighbouring farm, may add to their present small income some 100*l*. annually from Bee-farming. The fact is here; the *honey* taken from the combs by the Italian extractor is so limpid and clean that it is easy to obtain eighteen pence per pound for it; each hive in a dry summer will yield at a very low computation 80 lbs., thus 6*l*. is earned; and, as very little more labour is required to look after twenty hives than one, an income of 100*l.* annually is not a mere myth, a something impossible, but is feasible for any one at all industrious and painstaking.

Why, then, do so many farmers' wives and cottagers after a few years' experience of bee-keeping give it up in despair? "Oh! they don't pay." Many good reasons can be assigned why they do not pay. Here is one cause of failure: cottagers still use the common straw skep, all made of one shape and size, and exactly similar in appearance. These hives, sometimes to the number of a dozen, are arranged side by side, in a row, either exposed on a bench, or sheltered by the old-fashioned wooden beehouse. The young virgin queen, when out upon her wedding flight, in returning mistakes the hive, enters that in most cases next to her own, and is not allowed again to escape, but is invariably in a few minutes carried forth dead. In the spring the cottar's wife, when inspecting her apiary, expecting to see each stock flourishing, is astonished to find one half dead, owing in nine cases out of ten to the above cause.

But there are other things practised by cottagers which must always lead to failure. They often reply to the above question, "When the hives are taken up in the autumn we never find more than five or six pounds of honey in each, and it is not worth our while to bother with them, for in the swarming time we are compelled to watch incessantly, and the time thus lost is never repaid by our stocks." This results from the hives being too small.

I have each autumn for several years driven a great number of stocks for my neighbours, for the sake of the bees, with which I have improved my weak colonies, or built up new stocks, and I find the majority of the hives I have saved from the brimstone match have averaged 11 inches by 8 inches (inside measurement). Now, what can be expected from hives of this small size? If they possess a prolific queen, the cells, in all the combs except the two small outer ones, are always filled with brood in various stages of development; the room, in fact, is so limited that the queen watches for every vacant cell, and no sooner does the young bee leave it than it is again tenanted. They are prolific in one thing — that is, *swarms*. No wonder swarm after swarm issues, because the bees, becoming overcrowded, and having no room for honey storage, must either swarm or perish. To save themselves—for bees are often blessed with more foresight than their proprietors — they raise a queen and swarm. Again, what are the swarms really worth when they do come out? I have seen scores of swarms hived as separate colonies which would not, if measured, fill more than a pint. A pint of bees can do but little as a distinct stock.

Whilst other branches of rural economy have kept pace with the times, bee-keeping has been, and still is, retrograding amongst cottagers. There are not nearly so many apiaries now as in the days of our forefathers. How is it that bees flourish so well in a wild state in the vast primeval forests of America, so that when a stock is taken from a hollow tree it is not uncommon to secure an hundredweight of honey? Cottage bee-keeping can be made very profitable, if farmed in a proper manner; it will not only pay the rent of the labourer but find clothing also for his family.

The old-fashioned small skep must be abolished if success is to be secured. I do not wish to push any expensive bar-frame or costly hive upon my village friends; it can be done with the same, or less, outlay than at present. There are heaths in abundance on which the cheerful hum of the honey-bee is seldom heard, and hundreds of acres clothed with white Dutch clover, yielding the purest honey, are waiting to be kissed by the bee.

Cannot this state of things be remedied? We now import an astonishing quantity of both honey and wax from America, not reckoned by hundredweights but by tons, which ought to be produced at home to the benefit of our own land. Let us try to do it; but first the chief bee-keepers, who are cottagers, must be shown a better plan; then, finding it successful and worth their time and labour in a monetary point of view, they will not be slow learners. A further good will be gained; it will tend to keep the husband at home in the evenings, making and mending hives, or overhauling his stocks, instead of visiting the ale-house. The bee-bench has often had far greater attractions than the beer-bench.

THE SYSTEM OF BEE-FARMING.

Some fifteen years since, soon after the American Civil War, there came a rumour across the Atlantic from whence we import many hundreds of tons of honey that the system adopted by all the large bee-farmers in the Southern states was far different from the old-fashioned plan (still in use in this country), viz.: destroying the industrious workers when their season of toil is over in the autumn with the reeking fumes of the brimstone pit. The rumour, however, led to no results. Afterwards, we heard through a continental traveller, who had been making extensive inquiries in Italy, principally about the Ligurian or Alp bee, that the Italian method of bee-culture was one worthy of adoption, in fact the only way of making money out of bees. This differed very little from the American system.

We state these facts at the outset, because we lay no claim to originality, seeing ours is not a new or untried system of Bee-farming. Our hope and object is to persuade thousands of our own bee-keepers to begin Bee-farming, and not to be content with merely keeping a few stocks for their amusement. We are thoroughly satisfied that under this humane method thousands of stocks may be kept where we now find single ones in cottage gardens.

To come to the point. After keeping bees for nearly twenty years, and trying every plan we could hear of, we have learned one important fact, viz. bees will not thrive or do well, to say nothing of profit, if the hives be too large. It has become quite a rage with some apiarians, principally those who can afford to pay for their hobby, to have immense hives holding about 100 lbs. of honey. We have given this a patient and thoughtful trial; the result has been "immense loss from using the immense hives."

The only hive we have found successful is one not more than 12 inches square internally. This is taught us by the fact that our cottagers' wives who use the old-fashioned skep of about 12 inches square can generally succeed in having a fair honey harvest when their neighbours who employ large hives such as the Woodbury can seldom obtain much honey from them, except in unusually good honey seasons, which come round about once in five years. The cottager, however, destroys his bees in the autumn; this also is a ruinous system. What we want besides the right size of a hive is some way of taking the honey from the bees without destroying either the honey-gatherers or the comb in which it is stored. As the Italian method will do this—it is just the thing we are in need of. Now this system of Bee-farming rests upon the principle of not killing the goose which lays the golden eggs, or not destroying the comb for the sake of getting some 3 or 4 lbs. of honey out of it. Each of our small cottage hives would yield about

THE SYSTEM OF BEE-FARMING. 7

1 lb. of wax if the combs were all melted down. To manufacture this quantity of comb the bees have consumed 20 lbs. of pure virgin honey. The loss we thus sustain yearly is incalculable. It is a ruinous waste both of the honey and of the time required by the bees to manufacture it into waxen cells. Both the time and honey are saved by this homely plan of Bee-farming.

Having secured the right size of hive, the next point is to obtain a *honey-extractor*. There are several kinds of this machine in the market; ours, which will be fully described in a future page, is a cheap article as well as serviceable; if fairly used it will last and do the work of a large bee-farm for many years.

We advise all our readers never to use supers on the hive; let the bees manage their own affairs and send out swarms as often as they like. Placing supers on the top of the hive to secure a supply of virgin honey may seem to a novice very pleasant, but it deters the bees from swarming. Which is best,—a swarm that may be sold for ten shillings or more, and may be worth three times this sum to you, or two or three pounds of honey at the most? Our way never prevents swarming, for the bees, ever active and industrious, go on storing honey day by day; then the plan is this,—about twice a week, in the height of the honey season, puff a little smoke into the entrance of the hive, just to terrify them and make them quiet, then gently slip out the bar at each end of the hive, and having very carefully, if it happens to be sealed over, cut off the tops or caps over the cells by means of a sharp knife kept for the purpose, place it in the *extractor* in a cool place away from the hives; two or three whirls round completely empty it of all the honey; then give it back again to the bees; the comb not being in the slightest degree injured is again filled in three or four days, to be again emptied out. At each operation not less than *six pounds of pure limpid honey* comes out of the *extractor* clean and free from comb, &c. This is worth nine shillings, if sold privately. The honey being so pure, clean, and fresh, sells easily all the season round, which is not the case with the honey pressed out of the dirty comb, filled with decaying larvæ of the bees, &c. In fact, the black-looking autumn honey is of this description, and tainted as it is with sulphur it is a wonder that any one can think of eating it.

Our system, if followed honestly, should bring an annual income of ten pounds per hive. This perhaps is rather a high estimate, but in good honey seasons it will do more than this. In poor seasons it should clear six pounds. Taking swarms into consideration, as part of the profits of the bee-farm, we know of no trade so lucrative as that of a *bee-farmer*.

BEE-FARMER'S HIVE.

These being the general principles of our system, we proceed to treat them more fully in detail. And first of the character of the hive. We strongly urge this point to all who wish to become bee-masters, and not only bee-keepers; any one, even the most unskilled, can keep bees, but very few, alas! as our experience teaches us, are bee-farmers.

We should like to make all our readers first-class British bee-farmers, keeping, if circumstances would allow it, fifty hives in their apiary.

First, then, see to the hives; discard every hive over which you have not complete control. For instance, drones may increase to an alarming extent, so as to destroy the productiveness of the colony; you must be able at once to change the bars, and to place those bars containing drone-cells at the end of the hive, where the bees will only use them as honey-storers, and give up rearing any more drones. You cannot do this with a plain straw skep, the bees in these hives will have their own way in spite of you. Or your hive may be working badly, very few bees entering in or flying abroad; something is evidently going wrong, and the sooner you find it out the better; you may in our small bar-frame hives easily detect what is wrong. Smoke the stock, then pulling out the frames one by one you may find it is queenless; if so, a remedy is at hand; at once give them a bar from another hive containing eggs just laid; the bees will forthwith with joy commence to rear another queen and during the interregnum will work heartily as ever. If you are ever to make a good income from your apiary you must of necessity select bar-frame hives; with any other it is all up-hill work and constant loss.

We have stated the ruinous result of destroying the bees and combs every year just to obtain a few pounds weight of honey. To prevent this incalculable waste yearly, both in bees and treasure (combs), it will be needful to obtain a hive with frames easily removable, so as to take out the honey by means of the extractor.

The best hive, all points considered, is the bar-frame hive, often amongst British bee-keepers called the "Woodbury hive." There are many modifications of this hive, either in size, shape, the manner in which the frames are fixed, &c. such as Carr's improved Woodbury (this is too small, and from this cause alone worthless, if we have an eye to profitable Bee-farming), Siebert-on-the-Wold, Major Munn's bar-frame hive, Pettitt's bar-frame, Pettitt's temple-hive, Neighbour's new frame hive, Lee's octagon hive, Lee's Woodbury bar-frame hives, with straw sides, and others almost too numerous to mention.

By procuring a good well-made bar-frame hive, and carefully studying its construction, you may, if you can use a few joiner's tools, soon make as many as you require for your apiary. Others prefer to buy from some maker, and perhaps our readers will expect me to recommend a maker, but it would be wrong of me to recommend one before another. Try them, as I have done; procure their catalogue, or, what is better still, correspond with them; you will find them honourable men and most willing to give any information about hives, &c.

Having settled in our minds that wooden hives are in many respects superior to straw, then we must work the bar-frame hives; but first ask yourself this question, when commencing bee-keeping, "Shall I. work them so as to have a fair quantity of good super honey every season, or do I wish to increase my income from this source"? In th s latter case it will be better not to work them for supers.

Many persons who are in good circumstances keep bees for their own amusement; in this case they do not care whether they derive any profit or not; but, on the other hand, there are thousands, such as cottagers and agricultural labourers, who keep bees to procure a few extra blankets for the coming winter—in other words, they wish to make as much money by them as possible.

If you purpose keeping bees for amusement more than profit, and wish to make for your own table a little pure honey in the comb, then use only the ordinary bar-frame hives, which contain ten frames. When they exhibit signs of swarming, place a super, such as a neat bell-glass, on the top of the hive; the bees will immediately take to this, and, if the honey harvest is abundant, they will soon fill it with honey.

But those who keep bees, hoping to make a profit from them, I would strongly recommend not to attempt to work supers on their hives, but to follow my plan; think not of working supers, which are the common fashion of these days, but hive a large swarm in a bar-frame hive. For the first fortnight feed them liberally with syrup, which they will rapidly convert into wax for the combs: you will find the bees will repay this kindness with interest.

When the bees have filled the frames with comb, the queen will reserve the middle, or those frames situated in the centre of the hive, for breeding purposes, and the bees engaged in storing honey will make use of the frames on the outside; the queen might possibly breed in the outer frames, but I have not known of such a case in my experience. I have the top board on my hives made in three parts, so that I can remove the outer boards without disturbing the whole stock, or interfering with the breeding arrangements in the centre of the hive.

But a *chief point* is the size of the hive. Ask any bee-keeper who has had in use for any length of time the ordinary size of Woodbury hives—they all have a pitiful tale to tell: " Our bees do not seem to do well, we rarely see a swarm, and we gather but a small amount of honey from them." At this hour, from one end of England to the other, we hear only the cry—" Oh! bee-keeping is a poor paying game, we wish we had never seen them." The following fact, which recently took place, may, perhaps, be startling to some, it is nevertheless true. In one of our best conducted weekly magazines we saw advertised six hives with bees, &c. to be sold by a gentleman in the South of England. We wrote, asking price, kind of hive, and his reasons for thus selling his whole stock. His reply was to this effect: " My bees have cost me many pounds for hives, &c. I have also tried the Ligurian bee, a stock of which cost me 4*l*., thinking they would be better honey-makers, but my experience, if it is worth anything, is that they are nothing but a constant loss and vexation. I have only obtained eighteen pounds of honey the whole of last season. I had only one swarm last year, which I gave my man. I cannot tell how it is, they do me no good, for I have the best Woodbury hives, each containing thirteen bars; one of my neighbours, a poor widow, has cleared more than her rent last year from honey, and she keeps none but the common straw hives."

The above will afford us a lesson, if we only faithfully listen to its teaching. Here is a wealthy gentleman, who has given about 2*l.* each for his hives alone, yet he confesses he is sick of spending his money, and obtaining no return for his investment, while a poor cottager in the same village *does well*. Why? Because she has only hives, so far as size is concerned, just suited to the requirement of the bees; her bees are comfortable, they fill the hive with ease, swarm abundantly, and give her an abundant harvest, whilst her neighbour, with all his wealthy appliances, fails completely, because his hives are too large— the bees never fill them, they become dispirited, never swarm, and yield a poor return.

The words of Mr. Miner, an American bee-farmer, are worth listening to, for very few have had such extensive experience, or have kept such an enormous apiary :—

"Various are the reasons for making all hives of the same size. If we make them too *small* the bees are liable to perish from the effects of an unfavourable winter, in consequence of the weak condition of the family. The queen in such cases, as before stated, is curtailed of her necessary room, and not as many bees will be produced; and whatever operates as a check to the production of larvæ is a fatal error in the management of bees.

"If we construct our hives *too large* the bees will require two years to fill them, and the natural increase by swarming is lessened, and in some cases entirely prevented, for a series of years. Hives of this character are those made about fourteen inches in diameter, by about fifteen or eighteen inches in length. Such a size I consider to be opposed to the natural requirements of the bee

"When bees are placed in hives adapted to their natural wants, giving no excess of room, nor curtailing the use of such space as they actually require, they then cast off their first swarm of such numbers as nature teaches them are best adapted to prove prosperous, and it matters not how large your hive may be if a swarm be cast, which is seldom in families with large hives; it will not be in proportion to the size of the hive but in accordance with the laws of nature governing the bee.

"I have found, from many years of close application to the nature, economy, and general management of bees, that hives about one foot square in the clear, that is, in the inside, conform more to the natural habits and requirements of bees than any other size.

"In 1842 I had a few hives made 12 by 18 inches in the clear, that is 12 inches wide and 18 inches long. I found that it took the bees two seasons to fill my large hives, and, when filled, they did not swarm at all some seasons, for the reason that, however great may be the quantity of bees in the hive in the summer, they dwindle away before spring to a certain quantity, and thus leave a vacant space at the bottom of the hive of some six inches or more, to be filled up with the increase of spring, while smaller hives are full and are throwing off swarms in profusion. Here lies the philosophy of adapting the hive to the natural wants of the bee. I will illustrate this fact by a case.

"An apiarian placed a swarm of bees in a hive about 14 inches in diameter by 2 feet in length: the bees might possibly fill the hives with combs the second year, but swarming is entirely out of the question with a stock of bees in such a hive. The increase of every succeeding year disappeared before the spring following, since all the bees existing in hives in the spring of the year, save the queen, were the young of the preceding summer and fall. Now ten years have past, and this hive is in precisely the same condition that it was in nine years ago. Not a single swarm has ever issued therefrom. Ten generations of bees have existed, nine of which are passed away.

"We now pass to what would have been the result if the swarm had originally been put in a hive about twelve inches square.

"The second year a swarm would have issued without doubt, and perhaps two, but we will say one, in order to be on the safe side, as it is not my intention to give an overwrought picture in anything that I may discuss. We will now take the very reasonable and low estimate of one swarm from every stock every season, and count up how many would be the result at the end of ten years.

"The second year two in all; the third year four; the fourth year eight; the fifth year sixteen; the sixth year thirty-two; and so in the tenth year showing *five hundred and twelve families* from a single swarm!

"In this calculation we allow no drawbacks to the prosperity of the bees, such as destruction by foul brood, &c., yet the usual casualties attending the culture of bees I contend can be almost, if not wholly, prevented by proper management. So confident am I that 512 stocks of bees can in *ten years* be produced from a single swarm, that I should not hesitate to enter into heavy bonds (the uncertainty of life considered) to produce that number; or forfeit the whole actually produced.

"512 stocks of bees are worth at least five dollars per stock, amounting to the enormous sum of 2,560 dollars, while the same swarm, from which so vast a profit arises, if placed in too large a hive, at the end of ten years is worth but the paltry sum of five dollars, with no increase! I leave the reader to his own reflections on the wretched management of bees as too generally practised in every part of the country."

We can, from a single stock now in our own possession,

prove much of Mr. Miner's notes: the hive is an inch larger than the one he points out as a profitless size. We hived a large swarm into this box four years ago; it still remains in *statu quo;* no swarm has issued from it, nor have we had a single pound of honey from it, the population dwindles down every winter, and it takes them all the following summer to make good their heavy loss.

Neither is the picture an overwrought one. 576*l.* could be earned from the single colony and its yearly produce, and much more. Mr. M. does not say what could be realised from the honey harvest; this alone would probably be double the amount estimated; we generally have two good and early swarms from our hives, which, as will be seen, are slightly smaller than one foot square; still they are profitable—they are adapted to the requirements of the bees, and they return a rich reward for the labour.

Quinby, whose hives are much larger than ours, states as follows: "A hive 12 inches square inside, containing 1,728 cubic inches, has been recommended as *the best size*. This I think is large enough in many sections, as the queen probably has all the room necessary for depositing her eggs, and the swarms are more numerous and nearly as large as from much larger hives; there also is room sufficient for honey to carry the bees through the winter."

Quinby uses a bar-frame hive in his own apiary 12 inches deep by 19½ inches in length, and 12 inches in width. We have with care tested this hive, of which we had three made, but they never sent out a single swarm, and yielded a very small amount of honey; however, we would not blame Quinby for this, for he does not farm his stocks for the sake of swarms, or even hive honey; he endeavours to get as much super honey as possible, which he sends to the market in the comb. Again he states, and we are glad to have the testimony of this veteran bee-farmer in answer to those who condemn any hive in which the combs are not frequently renewed, "I can assure the reader *there is no profit* in the frequent renewal of the combs: all experienced and disinterested bee-keepers will bear testimony to this. I find it estimated by writers that twenty-five pounds of honey are consumed in elaborating about one pound of wax. This may be an over-estimate, but no one will deny that some is used. I am satisfied from actual experience that every time the bees are required to renew their brood-combs they would make from ten to twenty-five pounds of honey, hence I infer that their time may be much more profitably employed than in constructing brood-combs every year."

It is, we are glad to say, generally acknowledged by our best bee authorities that bees will store more in the stock-hive, *i.e.* in the hive in which the queen lives, and which is full of life and activity from being the dwelling-place of the working community, than in any other receptacle. In an excellent little catalogue of bee furniture just published by Mr. Yates, of Manchester, he makes the following admission: "It may be observed that bees

BRITISH BEE-FARMER'S HIVE.

storing the stock-hive increase in weight faster than when filling supers; the honey thus collected, however, is not so accessible." Mr. Yates is here speaking about the common straw skep, where it is quite true the honey *is never accessible*, but he admits a truth, which the sooner it is learned by every bee-keeper in the kingdom the better. There is no doubt about the rapid increase of weight in the loved home of the bees: the honey is there stored with a hearty will, because they are labouring for the honour and welfare of their queen. Now should you not deem a man to be very simple who carried all his earnings every week to the shed outside his own cottage home, placing it carelessly on a table, whence it is quickly taken away by some stranger? So the bees storing their treasure in a receptacle placed at the top of the hive called a super soon have it taken away by the bee-keeper. The super, whether it be in the form of a bell-glass or a small square wooden box placed at the top of the hive, in nine cases out of ten prevents swarming; thus it is *penny wise and pound foolish*. We have seldom sold a virgin swarm for less than twenty shillings, whereas if they store ten pounds of honey in the super it is thought to be very good. This is a wide difference in profit, besides the dreadful loss in honey, for it has cost your bees probably seven pounds of honey to manufacture the combs in which the paltry harvest is gleaned out of the super. What is this, then, to probably one hundred pounds stored in the stock hive? It is true you cannot reap so good a harvest yearly from each stock if the honey is not taken out of the hive as fast as it is stored, but this may be done far better by means of the honey-extractor.

Many foolish beekeepers place an *eke* at the bottom of the hive to make it larger, when the bees show signs of swarming; this results in the loss of the swarm, prevents any increase in the number of your stocks, and perhaps you are paid for the trouble by four ounces of beeswax, the chances being greatly against your having any honey in the new combs built at the base of the hive, for it is totally contrary to the habit of the bees to store any at the bottom of the hive. Surely you are willing to confess that your bees have a little common sense; they take the heavy honey as high up the combs as possible—if at the bottom, its weight would break off the tender waxen supports.

If you are wise you will never employ either the dreaded super or the eke in your apiary. If nothing else will teach you the heavy loss and dwindling stocks, year by year will bring our words to your remembrance, when too late.

Another system must be noticed, viz., that of collateral hives, that is, a hive placed at the side of the old stock, with openings made through the sides, where they join, so that the bees can take possession of it and use it for honey storage only. These have been tried by us until we were sickened by the total loss by death of two colonies, without any swarms for two summers, or even an ounce of produce, not to mention some ten pounds of syrup given each year to keep them from sheer starvation.

That our readers may not think us wrong in recommending hives so small as *less than a foot square* in the clear we here quote a few remarks of Dr. Bevan, a good old-fashioned English bee-farmer and writer on the honey-bee; one, moreover, who succeeded in keeping up a very large bee-farm. He had at one time not less, perhaps, than fifty-stocks, though he was years in discovering the simple secret. He says, " In a former part of this work a preference was given to those of Key's, but subsequent information and experience induce me to recommend their diameter to be three-eighths of an inch less than his, viz. " eleven and five-eighths inches square by nine inches deep in the clear."

The Bee Farmer's Hive is considerably larger than Bevan's; the only fault we have been able to discover in the latter is the absence of a moveable comb; without this it cannot be worked on our principle.

As far as we are able we now propose giving the exact

DETAILS OF THE BEE-FARMER'S HIVE.

measurement of the Bee Farmer's Hive, so that every reader may make them. We have during late years, not being ourselves very expert in the use of joiners' tools, had them made by a village carpenter, who charges us six shillings each for the complete hive, for a well-made straw-skep we have often given five shillings.

The inside measurement of the box containing the bars is twelve inches long, eleven and three-eighths inches wide, and ten inches deep. It has eight bar-frames, which rest upon grooves cut in the sides; these are exactly the size required by the bees for the brood-combs, seven-eighths of an inch in breadth, eight and a half inches deep, ten and a half inches wide, thus leaving about half an inch clear round the hive for the movement of the bees.

DETAILS AND MEASUREMENT OF THE BEE-FARMER'S HIVE.

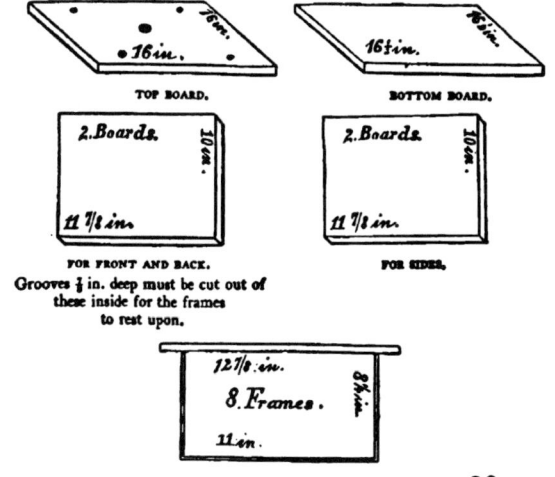

The six boards constituting the box must be made of inch deal well seasoned. The frames we employ are quarter-inch deal wood; they should be made to hang on the groove evenly. We use an ordinary turned wood door-handle for the feeding-hole in the top board, and above the entrance, in the front of the hive, we nail a small wood block, generally cut in a half-circle, to shield the bees from the weather.

To say they require no covering in the winter would be correct, still we prefer to place over each stock a common tea-chest, or, better still, to make *a few long hay-bands*, and twisting them around the hive to cover it at least three coils deep, then to place the tea-chest over this.

Many bee-keepers prefer not to paint their wooden hives. Well, our advice is, paint them both inside and out with not less than three coats, excepting only the bar-frames.

Just try an experiment the next winter, or during a whole year if you like. Keep a wood hive unpainted and by its side another covered well with stone-coloured paint. In winter you will observe the unpainted hive reeking with moisture exhaled by the bees; this to some extent cannot be avoided, even if good ventilation be carried out, but the painted hive will be quite dry, because the painted wood cannot absorb the water, which therefore gradually drains away or disappears through the open feeding-hole in the cover. An unpainted hive will crack under a hot sun, and insects will gradually but surely find a home and resting-place to breed in the crevices, but if these are all closed up by the hard lead-paint they never stop long, even if they do find an entrance into the well-guarded hive, and the painted hive *never cracks*. But the best test of all is the health of your colonies in the unpainted hive. Every bee-keeper will allow that his bees are not so hearty as in his painted hives.

Another test ought finally to settle this disputed point.

DETAILS OF THE BEE-FARMER'S HIVE.

How long will your unpainted hives keep in a condition fit for the stocks? Perhaps some two years; whereas our painted hives will wear for ten years, or even longer. Every spring we merely transfer the bars containing the entire stock, with comb, &c. to an empty hive, then scour the inside of the old hive well with soap and warm water. This is a little trouble, but is well repaid by the healthy hum of our stocks. Then, when the hive is thoroughly dried before the fire or in the sun, *but not before*, we again place the bees back again in their old home. By this plan we gain an insight into every stock, know its strength and condition, and, as *a stitch in time saves nine*, we can often avert some threatening disaster.

Immediately you obtain a new hive give it a good coat of stone-coloured paint, inside and out; when this is quite dry go over the same ground at least twice, then place it in the sun for a week or two, removing the cover-board; this will soon take away the peculiar turpentine odour, which, although probably not deleterious to the bees, yet may as well be removed before placing any stock in the hive. We then insert the bar-frames, and it is ready for the first swarm which issues.

Always remove the frames to some place of safety whilst the hive is being painted.

Another bit of warning may not here be out of place, because some of our bee-farming friends may not have much time in the busy season to read over our monthly notes, hence the more need of a word of caution in this place. Never after May arrives be without a few hives; you will not find it easy to have them made when a swarm is taking flight. As our American brethren say, *Nothing like being in readiness*. Remember, *your* stocks will swarm long before your neighbours if you adopt the Bee-Farmer's Hive; hence your special need of preparation.

MANAGEMENT OF BEE-FARMER'S HIVE.

This chapter will be very short, for it is intended chiefly for those who have hitherto only used the straw hives. The chief thing to be attended to is care at the outset. When the hive is newly stocked by a swarm they should be fed for a few days with syrup by means of the Lancashire feeder from the top of the hive. A great gain is thereby effected; a pound of syrup, costing about twopence, will make as much comb as a pound of honey worth eighteen-pence; but, should a succession of rainy days follow the hiving of the swarm, the gain is ten-fold. Many a good colony has been lost or dwindled down to almost nothing by the forgetfulness of the owner, when a little food at the outset would have saved all the loss.

Before stocking the hive be sure to run a little melted bees-wax along the upper part of the bar-frame. We use an old iron spoon, and melt the wax over a slow fire; then, holding the frame in the left hand, run the wax along it in a very thin stream; this will cause the bees to build their comb from a straight foundation.

Everything depends upon the even, straight combs. Every third day, therefore, puff a little smoke into the entrance, then remove the top board and gently take out each bar on which the bees have commenced building comb, and press the wax as straight as possible. *Never allow au uneven comb*; it wastes much space in the hive which could be profitably used either by the queen for rearing broods or for honey-storing by the workers. A very small amount of patience will conquer this difficulty; we need only say, it will cause you untold regret afterwards if this is not attended to in time, but, if the foundation of every comb is laid evenly and in a straight line at first, you may

MANAGEMENT OF BEE-FARMER'S HIVE.

with confidence trust the bees to build it evenly down to the base.

It is, moreover, impossible to use an uneven honeycomb in the Italian Extractor without breaking it; but the even comb is a perfect pleasure to place in the pan of the extractor; it comes out again perfect and clean from honey. After you have thus expended a little care on the foundations of the cells, no other care is needed; your bees will take to their comfortable home, and work with vigour to fill it with comb. This they accomplish in about a fortnight.

When taking out *each end-bar* to run through the extractor, do not disturb the central combs, for the queen is seldom seen away from the middle bars. A good plan is to keep *a soft hand-brush* in readiness, to brush off the bees from the comb into the hive when taking out the bars.

At the end of the honey-harvest, not later than 15th September, take out every bar in succession, carefully brush off the bees from each, and run the bars through the extractor. *Do not leave a pound of honey in the hive.*

Syrup will answer every purpose for winter food, and your bees will thrive as well upon it as upon honey. You will thus effect another large saving, which is not available in the straw-hives. You will have, probably, twenty pounds of good clean honey for sale, worth thirty shillings, and you give them in return five shillings' worth of sugar. When you commence to feed for the winter, give them about twenty pounds of good syrup, and at once make up the stock for the winter. To keep feeding for two or three weeks only unsettles the whole apiary, and leads to fighting and fearful losses. We feed each stock in about three days, then screw them up securely.

The question is sometimes raised whether it is best to keep each stock on a separate stand, or to put several side by side; we have no doubts about it. Keep each stock about three feet apart, on a stand of its own—it is far cheaper in the end. We should advise anyone just beginning bee-farming to adopt the small thatched bee-shed hereafter described, with just room enough for three hives, and have it so arranged that it may be easy to get to any side of the hive, whenever desirable; this can easily be enlarged, or another erected, when your stocks increase. Begin with two hives, and learn to manage these well first, then allow them to increase by natural swarming each season. It is well to have two or three hives always in readiness, that you may not have them to seek when wanted for a new swarm, for it is not easy to remove them after being hived for several days.

THICKNESS OF THE HIVES.

Some bee-farmers think a hive is a hive, and it matters not if it be thin or thick, of wood or of straw; we wish we could disperse this notion. Very much, we assure our readers, depends upon the protection given to the bees; no stock is more grateful for a little help.

Straw hives have many disadvantages—they are damp and liable to rot, and harbour enemies of the bee. The wooden-bar hive is the only one with which our system can be worked. The boards of the bar-hives should, if possible, be *one-and-a-half-inch in thickness*; the extra cost is not much. If your hives are not so thick then give them some other covering, especially during the prevalence of easterly winds. We wrap hay-bands around most of our stocks. The heat of the sun in summer is apt to melt the combs; in winter the cold often candies them and renders them useless; and in spring the thin hives neither retain the heat necessary for hatching the eggs nor for preserving the honey in a liquid state. Anyone may easily be convinced of this by laying some folds of linen on the top of the hive and then passing the hand between them, and there will be a degree of warmth felt, and therefore a loss of heat, which never happens when the hives are thick enough. They may be a little more costly, but the expense is more than repaid by the prosperity of your bees.

HIVE ENTRANCE.

It is of great importance to widen or contract the entrance according to the season or to the strength of the stock. Hives are weak in spring because the bees are occupied in the interior, keeping warm and taking care of the young, and the guard at the door is not strong enough to prevent intruders. Contract the door, therefore, and four bees will defend it better than thirty would if it were more spacious, and again enlarge it by degrees, according to the increase of the population. The workers must have room enough to go out and in without hindrance. When they begin to crowd together in groups at the entrance it is a sign of the interior being filled, and they should then have free access, as they will be strong enough to resist pillage. When the cluster becomes very large, which it will do as the drones increase, enlarge the entrance as much as possible. It is even desirable sometimes to open the hive a little at the top in order to moderate, by a current of air, the excessive heat that forces the bees to the outside. After the destruction of the drones the population diminishes, and the bees no longer cluster outside, and then is the time to begin again to contract the entrance in order to prevent plunder.

For this purpose we use little wooden wedges, which cost nothing, as anyone may make them with a knife and bit of stick. They help to protect the bees from the moths, which make sad havoc when once they gain access to the hive. They deposit their eggs in the interstices between the cracks in the hives, and are soon hatched by the heat. In the fine weather of April and May the hives should be most carefully and frequently overhauled to prevent the moth gaining an entrance into them.

A little care in looking after the entrance is never lost. Many bee-farmers overlook it as a trivial thing until injury is done by robbers, or some other sly enemy, which comes unperceived, and as slily works dreadful mischief.

BRITISH BEE-FARMER'S HONEY-EXTRACTOR.

The simple honey-extractor which we figure below is the best and most efficient that we have ever known. The large and cumbrous wooden machine, first introduced from Germany several years ago, and costing about 5*l.*, is too expensive for the large class of cottage bee-keepers in this country; it is also too big and unwieldy for the class of bee-farmers we represent. We have seen one which would occupy the whole of a cottage parlour when in use, but the one we now bring before the notice of our readers can easily be made by any tin-worker, and costs only a few shillings.

The body of the extractor is made of tin. It is merely an inverted cone open at the base or neck, which, when in use, is kept tightly closed with a cork; the handle is made of iron, with a rounded bend at the upper part.

Closely fitting on the cone is the box (page 27) prepared for the comb; we fasten this on the cone by means of a long piece of wire, so that the lid and afterwards the box itself is securely fastened on the machine. The lower part of the box, on which the comb rests, is made of stout wires soldered on the tin edge about one quarter of an inch apart, to allow the honey to run through

BEE-FARMER'S HONEY-EXTRACTOR.

into the lower portion. This should be loose, so that it can be cleaned.

Any expert tinman can from our description and figures

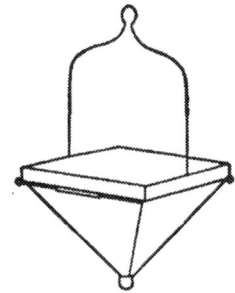

BEE-FARMER'S HONEY-EXTRACTOR (CLOSED).

make it, but when the order is given care must be taken to have the size of the box correct. This would be secured by having it made to the size of the bars in use in the apiary, allowing, of course, for the extra thickness of the combs. It is well to fix or to solder a piece of fine copper-wire netting about four inches above the neck. This will act like a sieve, and cause the honey to run from the machine perfectly clear and free from comb and other impurities.

HONEY-EXTRACTOR (BOX OPEN).

The original of the Bee-Farmer's Honey-Extractor is the Italian "*Smielatore*." We have made several valuable improvements, however, upon the Italian machine, which is scarcely available for our system of bee management.

Years ago we were wishing to meet with some cheap machine, such as the Bee-Farmer's Extractor, but we searched in vain; now no one need complain, for we have a *cheap* machine, *easy* to work, *cleanly* in use, and a great advance upon the old system. Only one is required for a large apiary; it can be cleansed with boiling water in a few seconds, and it is at once ready for use.

HOW TO USE THE EXTRACTOR.

Of course, the Extractor can only be used with the bar-frames, such as are found in the Bee-Farmer's Hive. Before commencing to use the machine gently smoke the hive at the entrance, then unscrew the top-board, first removing one bar at the end of the hive, and carefully replacing the top-board. Fix this in the machine, and, having removed all the honey from both sides of the bar-frame, replace it in the hive, and take away the frame at the other end of the hive. The only care needed is not to break the comb, for this cannot well be repaired, and results in heavy loss of honey and time, and do not be rash or hasty in your movements when removing the frames from the hive, but do it so gently that the bees will scarcely perceive their loss; in fact, our experience has been that the bees begin to store it again with honey in about an hour after it is returned to the hive. Before placing the comb in the box cut off the caps over the cells with a sharp knife and place the *cut side first* on the wire grating, then fix the machine in the ring of the handle of a long house-brush or anything similar; now it only remains

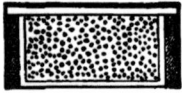

HONEY EXTRACTOR (COMB AS IT APPEARS IN THE BOX).

to turn the machine rapidly *in one direction*, and the whole of the honey on the one side of the comb will run out into the lower part of the machine; afterwards turn the comb and repeat the process.

The best plan of using the Extractor is to place a large staple in a blank wall or door of any shed; then, if another be fixed to the end of the broom-handle, the machine can be worked far better and by a single hand; but, if it is used without the iron staple, it will be necessary for some friend to help by holding one end of the handle and working in unison.

We should advise the bee-keeper to practise *the swinging* of the machine before placing the comb in the box; he will thus have more confidence, and probably avoid breaking the comb.

Carefully wash every part of the Extractor before putting it away after using it. This caution is the more needful because the bees would soon find it out by the flavour of the honey, and thus become household pests instead of household pets.

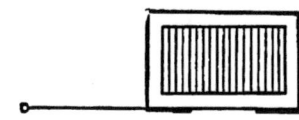

HONEY EXTRACTOR (WIRE BARS ON WHICH THE COMB RESTS).

You can take out the frame at each end of the hive about every fourth day and pass them through the extractor. Each time we have an average of four pounds of pure clean honey, requiring no straining afterwards, which will realise about six shillings. Remember, nothing is so saleable in the honey-market as clean limpid honey, and this you secure constantly the season through. A friend, to whom we introduced the system, writes, stating, "I have now hives yielding me twelve shillings weekly from four to six weeks of the season, and about six shillings for another three weeks, besides about fifteen pounds of pure honey at the end of the season, which I exchange for cheap syrup. Before I introduced the Extractor I got a very poor return in my apiary."

Now is not this a more sensible plan than the one adopted by nearly every cottage bee-keeper simply because their fathers did the same, that is, letting the bees work the season through and then cruelly murdering the whole colony for the sake of about twelve pounds of sulphur-tainted honey?

We may be pardoned if we draw attention again to the striking fact that the bees must each year first gather twenty pounds of honey before they can make the wax needed to build up a small cottage-skep with combs. A method which saves all the old combs, and, after taking out the honey, gives them back to the hive to be again filled, plainly effects an immense saving. The Bee-Farmer's Bar-Frame Hive will take about twenty-three pounds of honey to fill with comb; after it is once filled, no more loss is caused ever afterwards. The whole time of the stock is taken up solely with honey-collecting, with the results stated above. *If you only use the extractor once in the season it will repay its cost.*

WHEN TO COMMENCE BEE-FARMING.

Various opinions prevail amongst bee-writers on this subject; some are very misleading, and many beginners in bee-farming have cause to regret ever following the advice given. The generality of writers have advised those who are about to start an apiary to purchase stocks in spring. We, on the contrary, assert it is far better to secure stocks about the month of September. The reason why so many

WHEN TO COMMENCE BEE-FARMING.

recommend spring is, that, the winter being past, they have got over the worst part of the year and have the whole of the summer before them; but they forget that a hive which may be had for 20*s.* in the autumn will cost 30*s.* in the spring, so that a great saving is effected by purchasing stocks in the autumnal months.

To thousands of bee-keepers the most disagreeable part of the work is taking up hives for the honey, and they would prefer to sell the stocks for a trifle, taking the honey, of course, at a fair valuation. Keep a sharp look-out amongst the cottage bee-keepers in your neighbourhood— the earlier the better; tell them you wish to secure a few stocks of bees, and you will soon meet with any quantity if they have not commenced taking up the hives. Then, as to the price. Five shillings is a fair valuation for the stock if it is in a plain skep-hive. You may weigh them if you prefer, and agree as to the rate per pound for the honey, and pay accordingly. It is, perhaps, the safer plan to leave the hive on the old stand until the bees are settling down for the winter before removing them to their new home. If you purchase hives in the spring after the flight has commenced you run the danger of losing one-half the inmates, especially if they are only removed a short distance from the old stand, for they will invariably fly back to the place, and thus miserably perish.

Do not attempt to remove the bees to a new hive. We advise what we know to be for the good of those who are inexperienced. Remove the stock with the old hive in the autumn; then, if you judge by the weight they have not sufficient food for the winter, cut a hole in the top of the hive so as to be able to feed them liberally with syrup by means of the Lancashire Bee-Feeder, which we should recommend everyone to obtain beforehand.

Leave the stocks in the old skep in which you purchase them until they have swarmed. Before you expect the first swarm to go off procure a Bee-Farmer's Hive and hive the swarm into it. This will be far better than placing the old stock in the new hive, for the swarm, being nearly all young bees, are full of vigour, and therefore lose no time in filling their new domicile with comb.

A few homely hints will here be useful. *First*, take care you are not purchasing "a pig in a sack." Examine carefully if *all the drones are dead*. In most cases you can easily ascertain this by observing all around the bee-bench. In every vigorous stock the drones should now be all dead, and they will be seen lying on the ground before the entrance of the hive. If any of these gentry are seen buzzing about and taken freely into the hive as old friends, have nothing to do with the stock, for the certainty is, it is a queenless colony, therefore valueless, except for the honey. Another point must not be overlooked. You are liable, if inexperienced, to have old stocks foisted upon you. Puff a little smoke into the entrance of the hive, then lift it gently from the stand and examine the combs. If they are *black and dirty-looking* refuse the stock, because by this simple test you are sure it is an old colony, and it may prove to be worthless in the coming season; but, if the combs are a fresh-looking straw-colour, it is a young stock. Secure it as a prize. Before buying them, however, go some dull rainy day. If you observe the bees flying about briskly have a care what you are doing. Bees in a good condition will be quiet in such weather, but others in a starving state will be compelled to forage as best they can. As the *golden rule* is, have strong stocks, it would be advisable to see that the colony is strong before taking them home. A poor stock seldom proves useful.

Let it be with your bees as with a wife, "never take them on the recommendation of another person." The advice given by Wildman is very good: "The person who intends to erect an apiary should purchase a proper number

WHEN TO COMMENCE BEE-FARMING.

of hives at the latter end of the year, when they are cheapest. The hives should be full of combs, and well stocked with bees. The purchaser should examine the combs in order to know the age of the colony; the combs of that season are white, those of a former year are darkish yellow, and when the combs are black the hives should be rejected, because old hives are more liable to vermin and other accidents." As to the weight; your stock should not weigh less than fifteen pounds without the hive. Of course, a few words are here necessary. Do not think because they are much lighter that they are also worthless. It is a very easy method to feed them up to the requisite weight, but do not allow them to commence the winter without fifteen pounds of food at the least. We make a syrup by gently simmering *three pounds of best lump sugar* with *two pounds of rain-water*. Do not be afraid to cut a small hole, say 2 inches in diameter, in the crown of a straw hive; it is a simple plan for feeding them.

A few words are needful about transferring a swarm to the frame-hives. We always hive them first in a straw skep which we keep for the purpose, then knock them out on the top of the bars. Immediately they have settled they should be removed without loss of time to the stand you intend them to occupy permanently. It is well the moment after knocking the swarm upon the bars to throw a tablecloth over them for about half-an-hour; for, if the topboard is put on before they have gone down or have clustered on the frames, a great number may be killed.

MODERN BEE-HIVES.

During recent years, owing to the knowledge of the requirements of bees, or rather from the many practical experiments on the economy and the working of the hive, as well as from the extensive and widespread knowledge of the habits of our domestic bees, numerous useful hives have thus come gradually into use. Some few of these modern hives we have pleasure in introducing to the notice of our readers. There are many bee-farmers who believe strongly in them, because they have, from the best of all motives, found them successful in their apiary. Many of our western bee-keepers, whose friendship we esteem highly, work the Woodbury. One note of warning must be given. Endeavour to have the hive in use on your bee-farm as near *one foot square* in the clear as is possible; our reasons, given in a previous page, should be carefully read. We do not recommend one hive before another. A very good plan is to send, or write, for a catalogue of hives, &c. from any of the chief dealers in such articles; such as Messrs. Neighbour, High Holborn, London; Mr. Pettitt, of Dover; and Mr. S. Yates, seed-merchant, Old Millgate, Manchester. If any difficulty should arise, any of the above excellent firms are ever ready and willing to give advice.

NEIGHBOUR'S GLASS WOODBURY HIVES.

Most advanced bee-keepers are now tolerably conversant with the Woodbury bar-frame hives, either practically or by report. It is a bar-frame hive, and may be described simply as a wooden box fourteen and a half inches square, inside measurement, and nine inches deep. The usual ten frames fill up this space, resting upon a rabbet a little below the surface, leaving a space of three-eighths of an inch between the upper side of the bars and the crown (top) board. This allows a free passage for the bees on the top. Each frame, as recommended by the Devonshire Bee-Keeper, is seven-eighths of an inch wide; the frames hang in the rabbet so as to leave three-eighths of an inch from the floor-board; in fact, if properly made, a free passage is allowed for the bees on all sides.

NEIGHBOUR'S GLASS WOODBURY HIVES.

For many years British bee-farmers thought any hive containing more than ten frames was hurtful to the bees and could not be worked successfully. We should be only too glad to learn that this opinion was gaining ground, for hives on the Woodbury system are being manufactured and sent out with twenty frames, and in the hands of inexperienced persons they turn out most disastrously.

GLASS WOODBURY HIVE.

The glass hive, of which we give an illustration, is manufactured by Messrs. Neighbour, of High Holborn. They describe it as follows:

"Some bee-keepers like to be able to make a full and daily inspection of the hive; we have therefore constructed a hive of wooden frames, inclosed on all sides and on the top with glass. The divisions are precisely the same as the ordinary Woodbury. The crown has a round hole cut in the glass to admit of feeding. The four sides are constructed of double glass to preserve the bees from variations of temperature."

Many persons believe these hives—which are very elegant, of stained oak, and varnished—will not answer as a winter residence for the bees, but if they have a wooden covering on all sides, the same as used to shield the other hives from the weather, bees will winter in them and come out early in the spring hearty and strong. Our experience has taught us that damp kills far more bees than cold. The top board should be propped up about one-eighth of an inch all the winter to allow the moisture to escape: this is all that is necessary.

These hives are well adapted for the villa garden, for the more timid part of the fair sex may inspect them at any time with confidence. As a hive for the lawn, to give intellectual amusement to visitors, this kind is certainly the most suitable.

COTTAGE HIVES.

As many still prefer the simple homely hive of their fathers, we have given illustrations of several that we have ourselves found useful, and which are about the best size for bee requirements. We do not, however, recommend their adoption, but give them as useful to those who will not change their old-fashioned plan.

PETTITT'S IMPROVED STRAW HIVE.

There are three straw hives sold by dealers in apiarian requisites which very closely resemble each other. Were we to listen to the high encomiums lavished on them by their respective inventors we should feel inclined to purchase all the series. However, we hope our readers after reading these notes will be persuaded to try only one, which they can afterwards so modify as to be equal to any cottage hive.

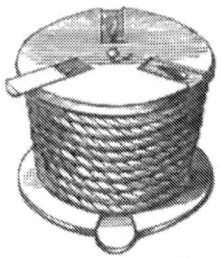 

PETTITT'S IMPROVED COTTAGE-HIVE.

This hive is as above figured, with an ordinary inch board, in which are three openings closed with zinc covers sliding in a groove cut in the wood; over these holes one or more honey-glasses can be placed at the will of the bee-keeper in early spring. A straw cap is used to cover the top with the honey-glasses; a common straw skep will answer the purpose. This hive possesses all the requisites of a good cottage hive.

Milton's Cottage Hive is similar to the above, and, when Mr. Milton introduced it to the apiarian world in 1846, it was thought to be so useful, and withal such a first-class honey-making hive, that he gained the Ceres Medal from the Society of Arts. The only real difference in either size or style is that, instead of having only one board fastened on the straw, it has two, the upper one being made to revolve on an iron pivot. When the honey-glasses or supers are filled, instead of sliding in the zinc to shut out the bees the upper cover is turned round, and the bees are effectually prevented from gaining access to the supers; but this point is gained with much less expense and trouble by using the zinc slides. Mr. Bevan Fox several years since made a slight modification upon the above, which was made public in the pages of the Gardener's Chronicle. The openings through the cover to the supers are usually made round, but Mr. Fox pointed out the great advantage of having them cone-shaped (*e.g.*, one end being sharply-pointed), so that when the zinc slides are pushed in to exclude the bees before removing the honey-glasses the bees are gradually urged out of the way. If it be done slowly by winch the risk of crushing or destroying the bees is reduced to a minimum.

The hives are certainly very reasonable in price, and, best of all, they can easily be manufactured by anyone possessing a little ingenuity.

PETTITT'S COTTAGE HIVE.

To those persons who cannot spare much time in the management of their stocks, such as cottagers who are out working all the day, and have only a few minutes in the evening to glance round their bee-bench, this hive will be a boon.

PETTITT'S COTTAGE HIVE.

Those who are ingenious enough may easily manufacture a few *caps*, or supers, during the long winter evenings, and use them on their common skeps, by cutting out two inches from the crown. When the bees show signs of swarming by clustering outside, at once place the super on the hive. It may prevent swarming, but you will have instead a few pounds of superior, or super-honey, which is worth 1*s*. 6*d*. per pound.

We can also recommend this hive. We found it very successful, both in producing fine swarms and giving a fair yield of honey. The super however did not succeed.

NARBONNE HIVE.

When visiting the South of France several years ago we received a most courteous letter from an English medical practitioner, urging us not to forget to make a diligent search when at Narbonne for their hives, and to be sure to bring home again a good report, so that the same system might be adopted in Cheshire. The bee-keepers in the South of France are very careful to secure excellent honey, though they secure a limited quantity only. A large supply seems to come to the English market from the neigbourhood of Narbonne, judging from the sale in this country of what is called Narbonne honey by Italian warehousemen and chemists; those however who have travelled on foot over the Narbonne district, as we have done, declare that but few bees are kept compared to what we see about cottages in England.

When over there we inquired both about the hive in use and the honey supply. The best honey is gathered very early in the season, when the bees visit the wild rosemary (Rosmarinus officinalis, L.), which is most abundant on the extensive hills to the right of the town, more plentiful than the gorse (Ulex nanus) on our heaths. All this early honey is sent off and sold at a high price. The second harvest is very inferior in quality.

The hives are not unlike the Grecian, except that they are smaller, and taper from the summit more gradually downwards, whereas the Grecian is very wide at the part where the wooden bars are fixed. A common English skep could easily be converted into a Narbonne Hive.

Cut off the top and fix a piece of wood to the sides with spaces cut out by a hand-saw resembling bars, in the Woodbury Hives, for the bees to attach the combs, at the will of the bee-keeper. To those fond of experiments with hives it may offer an inducement to make one for trial.

IMPROVED NARBONNE HIVE.

To cottage bee-keepers, or gardeners, who have little spare time at their disposal just when the honey harvest is the most abundant, these would prove very interesting hives if made with a window at the back to allow the operations of the inmates to be occasionally watched.

YATES'S ROUND-TOPPED HIVE.

Mr. Yates, seedsman, of Manchester, has acquired celebrity for his straw-skeps, and many Lancashire bee-keepers, especially those who follow Pettigrew's theory, are almost compelled to purchase their skeps from Messrs. Yates, because no one else can furnish straw hives of the size required.

YATES'S ROUND-TOPPED HIVE.

This illustration will give our readers a tolerable idea of the shape of the hive, but to look at a hive twenty inches in diameter, and fourteen inches high, both inside measure, is enough to astonish an old-fashioned apiarian. It certainly is an enormous hive, and, best of all, when it comes to be taken off the stand in the autumn, if tolerably well filled with pure honey, it will certainly hold not less than eighty pounds.

We, however, draw our readers' attention to Yates's hives not so much for their size as for their excellent workmanship; we believe they are manufactured in Scotland, and we honestly confess we never saw any straw hives so strongly made as these. To show their durability, we had one in use for over four years, and it then seemed as if it would last four more, but if a common skep lasts two years it is thought to have done its duty.

Another feature about this hive is the improvement in the moveable wooden top, worked in the straw; the plug we have found very convenient both for supering and feeding. Hives of Pettigrew's pattern are also sold by Mr. Yates. These differ in having a flat top with a straw plug in the centre. We do not recommend a flat top hive for the simple reason that when an ordinary sized swarm is introduced they commence the formation of the combs at the side, or often in the corners, thus the combs are all irregular and unevenly built, which hinders both the breeding and honey storing; in other respects they are excellent skeps.

What we chiefly want is the small cottage skep, about twelve inches square internally, as strongly made as those of Yates's pattern; we have seldom seen these monster hives do any real service as honey-hives, but rather the reverse.

REMOVING SUPERS FROM THE HIVE.

Many bee-keepers experience great difficulty when removing their supers at the close of the season, about August, to get rid of the bees, for they seem most reluctant to quit the richly-laden combs. Sometimes we are recommended to place them in a shady part of the garden at a distance from the apiary, when finding out the loss of their queen they rapidly leave the super. We have done this to find in a few hours all the honey taken out of the combs by robber bees far cleaner than I could have performed the operation.

Mr. Cheshire exhibited a little contrivance at the Crystal Palace Honey Show which attracted much attention, and we have since found it most useful. It is a simple trap, which, whilst allowing the bees to escape, prevents them from again entering the super if ordinary care be exercised. It can be made in a few minutes by even a lady amateur.

First, procure a box sufficiently large to contain the supers, and bore two or three quarter-inch holes in its side; over these place a pin exactly in the centre, which is kept in its place by two other pins placed just beneath the head, and two at the point. The bee pushes up the central pin to escape, but the pin again closes the hole against an entrance. The box should have a tight-fitting lid to exclude all light except that admitted through the quarter-inch hole. The annexed illustration will explain its working, and also show

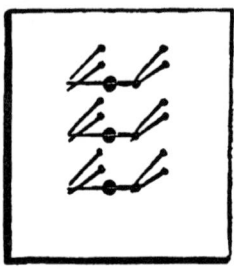

CHESHIRE'S BEE-TRAP.

how easily it can be put together. An ordinary half-inch board, planed, may be converted into the "five-pin bee-trap"—a name given to it by Mr. Cheshire—or even thick cardboard can be made to answer. We have found the common American cheese-boxes, which can be purchased from any provision dealer in market towns for two pence each, useful for small honey glasses (supers) such as those sent out with Neighbour's Cottage Hives.

HOW TO MANUFACTURE STRAW HIVES.

These hives, more commonly known as "skeps," are not difficult to make, and are very simple in their con-

HOW TO MANUFACTURE STRAW HIVES.

struction. To make them will both save trouble and expense. In many villages at some distance from a market-town it is often impossible to procure them just in a moment at swarming time, when they are frequently required without a moment's warning.

Straw skeps are now much higher in price than they were. A few years ago they might be purchased for a shilling, now they are double that price, and gardeners and labourers in gardens who love their bees, but have not much money to throw away upon hives, would gladly in the long winter evenings prepare skeps for the coming season if they knew how to do so. The annexed illustration will, at a glance,

SKEP MAKING.

explain how to make them; only two articles are necessary, straw, and either a few long bramble stems, or, what is far better, a few long canes, which may easily be procured in town.

The straw should be wheat straw, and as long as possible. We have always found hand-threshed straw superior for this purpose to machine-threshed, because the latter is bruised and broken, so as frequently to be worthless. The cane should be split up carefully into thin strips.

Many makers use a cow's horn to work the straw through in plaiting the hive, but a circular bit of tin soldered so as to keep the straw of an even thickness in the plaits is more convenient and useful; the tin should be a little wider at one end than the other.

At first great care must be taken in preparing the first round or plait to make it very firm and strong, because on this depends in a great degree the quality of the hive, and all the weight rests upon this. If this is performed satisfactorily the greatest difficulty is overcome, and the remainder is comparatively easy work.

Much may be learned by first taking in pieces an old hive, and observing the fastenings of the cane as well as the mode of its working.

The hive entrance is cut out after the hive is completed.

HIVE BONNETS.

We have seen many different kinds of covers for bee-hives in various parts of England, such as cracked washing-mugs, potato boxes, guano and other kinds of bags and sacks, old buckets, often with a stave missing; tins of all shapes and sizes, as hand-boards, galvanised iron buckets, especially when they have become so leaky as to be worthless for any other purpose; slates, and I have even seen a two-gallon ale bottle, minus the mouth and handle. It would be impossible for us to enumerate all the covers we have seen in cottage gardens over hives, which are placed singly, each on a separate pedestal or stand, undoubtedly the best method of placing bees. Well-to-do farmers, when bees are kept for the sake of profit, have, as a rule, bee-benches of wood, sometimes ornamentally built by the village carpenter; and we have seen them with the sides built of bricks, with a slated roof: these cannot be too strongly condemned; but we have been grieved to see in hundreds of cases no covering at all placed over the skeps.

No wonder bee-keeping is so often condemned as profitless. Thousands of stocks are either starved or drowned out, owing to carelessness or want of thought. More stocks are annually lost from this cause than from any other.

Cottagers in our day are often thankful to learn any new improvement in bee-keeping, as witness the fact that many are now employing their spare moments in making the Woodbury bar and frame hives. Proceeding recently past a neat lodge, occupied by an industrious couple, and connected with one of the large residences in the North of England, I was pleased to observe a new plan or method for covering the old-fashioned straw skep. In the well-kept garden surrounding the lodge were about half-a-dozen stocks of bees scattered here and there, but arranged so as to have plenty of sunlight, and, best of all, surmounted with a rustic cover to keep the industrious inmates free from the dreaded rainfalls. We may add, they were to us the prettiest object in this neatly-arranged and clean garden.

For the advantage of my cottage friends I will, in as few words as possible, describe how to make these hive-bonnets.

Most cottage bee-keepers have children; if so, during play-hours they should be induced to glean the neighbour-

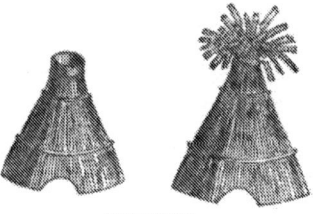

SKEP BONNETS.

ing wheat fields after all the corn has been carted by the farmers. We advise gleaning because threshed straw is unsuitable, and will not make good rain-proof covers, for the stalks of wheat, after passing through the machine, are often much crushed and bruised. Barley and oat straw may answer, although not so serviceable as wheaten straw. First procure as long straw as possible, and grasp as much with the left hand as will cover one hive when equally spread out. Grasp it just beneath the ears, not the root end, and tie it tightly with strong whipcord passed several times round it; then take an empty skep, exactly of the same size as those containing the bees, and place the tied straw over it, spreading it out of an equal thickness all round; now make a band (a small cane split down the centre will make two), pass the band over the straw so as to fit rather closely about the middle, and saturate the straw with water, at the same time press the uneven parts with a flat piece of wood. When dry it will be stiff, so as to lift off and preserve its shape, although it is well to tie on the cane with thin twine, which only requires a little patience. Trim it neatly round with the scissors, leaving an arched entrance for the bees. The tuft of ears at the summit may either be cut off or, when the wheat is knocked out, left as an ornament. We prefer the latter, it has a better effect. Sometimes they are painted stone colour, with two coats of paint, and with careful usage they will last for several years.

RUSTIC BEE-SHEDS.

Quite as many opinions prevail about bee-stands and bee-houses as are to be met with about bee-hives. Whilst one person advocates keeping the stocks on distinct stands, another fancies it is better to have a splendid house made for his bees, so that he can place about ten hives "all in a row," but every hive touching each other. So far as keeping bees on distinct and separate stands, so that the hives are not less than three feet apart, no one can be a

RUSTIC BEE-SHEDS.

greater advocate for it than myself; but another thought comes before us, they must be sheltered in the winter or suffer loss. Then, if they are in straw hives and you place (say) an ordinary pan-mug over them to shelter them from rain, &c., you run the risk of finding both hives and bees rotting from the moisture of the winter. If they are in a shed open on all sides, with a free circulation of air, they come out in the spring healthy and vigorous, and quite prepared for the hard work of the honey-gathering season; but we have never yet found any hive healthy which was closely shut up all the winter free from air or ventilation, and after frost reeking with moisture.

The annexed illustration is a plain rustic shed. It placed at the corner of the garden, and covered neatly with sedges or rushes, it will prove an ornament to any garden or shrubbery. The one we have seen had a bench running the whole length in the centre, made to hold five hives. This is certainly more economical than placing them singly on separate stands, and may be adopted at the will of the apiarian.

Other bee-farmers use plain wooden sheds covered in on all sides. These harbour insects and mice, which will sooner or later prove a sad pest; and not only so, for the bees we have kept in this way were never so healthy or so profitable as when in the open shed.

Our rustic bee-shed is open on all sides; it should have

RUSTIC BEE-SHED.

three posts at the back but only two in the front, one at each corner, for it is advisable to put no obstacle before the hive. Strong laths are sufficient for a foundation for the cover, which may be either straw, thatch, or reeds. The common river-sedge (Scirpus maritimus, L.) is the best; it has a much neater appearance than straw, and, if the shed is designed as an ornament, by all means use reeds, sedge, or the still more common rush (Juncus communis, L.) On the score of cheapness little need be said. If suitable timber is at hand a pound will go far towards completing the structure; on the other hand, if one of the splendid bee-houses (so-called) is purchased from a dealer in apiarian furniture, a good durable house will cost not less than 15*l.* Having had extensive experience in our own and neighbouring apiaries we cannot too strongly condemn all such houses.

Again, if a separate wooden cover is made for each of the hives it will be very expensive. Let us then persuade all our friends to have an open shed.

Many may object that the keen winds of winter with bitter sharp frosts may injure the bees. It is not cold that injures the stocks, but, as we have shown before, the wet and moisture after a thaw. A free passage for the air through the hives, whether they be of wood or straw, will keep them free from damp, and the bees are healthy.

One inducement to preserve the stocks in open sheds is, that they consume far less honey during the winter, for, when kept in an unnatural, warm, or damp atmosphere, they are continually eating; but if they are kept in a natural condition, such as we can imagine their state in the tree-stems of the primeval forests, the contrary is the case. If the wood hives are of sufficient thickness, and the stand is in a sheltered position, it may be enough to cover in the hive itself, though we recommend in every case when convenient to provide some warm covering, such as old sacking, or a tea-chest placed loosely over the hive.

We have found that our hives which have had strong hay-bands wound round them during the whole winter have wintered the best. This is a simple and cheap covering, besides being within the reach of every bee-farmer.

SITUATION OF THE APIARY.

Whether the hive be towards the west or south is a matter of no moment, but the situation is everything; no care can atone for an error here.

The hives must above all things be sheltered from the wind. A wall, however high, or a simple hedge, is not sufficient, because the bees that fly to the fields prefer stopping in places where the air is tranquil, near bushes, or along hedges or dells, where they find a much greater abundance of honey than in places exposed to gales of wind. They fatigue themselves flying from flower to flower, and still more returning to their home after having completed their little work. With a rapid flight they get over a great extent of space, frequently against the wind; but on approaching the hive they slacken their speed and advance, wheeling round and round to find or recognise it. A mistake at this time might be fatal and cost them their lives; and if at this moment they encounter a strong current of air, or a whirlwind repels them, they are again forced to wheel round to reconnoitre their habitation. After a hard struggle the most vigorous arrive; the others fall without power to rise again, especially when the air is cold or the sky clouded. The ground will then be strewn with dead or dying bees, which *never happens when the hives are placed in sheltered situations.*

Again, a common belief prevails that hives will not do well unless they stand in the sun. This is an error. Bees like the shade when working, and like the sun only when in the fields; it then animates and sustains them. For this reason, when people wish a swarm to settle after it has left the hive, they hasten to cover it, because the shade induces them to rest, while a hot sun annoys them and induces them to take flight again. When we wish to disperse a cluster of bees off the front of a hive, we have only to expose it to the rays of the sun in the heat of the day. The bees then retreat under the hive, on the side, or behind it. They thrive well in thick forests and delight in them, because there they find a uniform temperature and a propitious shade. Often during the dog-days we have seen the honey running out and the combs melting in hives exposed to the heat of the sun. In one hour sometimes a whole apiary will be destroyed. It is also a mistake to suppose hives exposed to the sun produce the earliest and strongest swarms. We have oftener than once experienced quite the reverse. Our earliest swarms have generally come from the hives which are best shaded and only receive the sun late. We have even lost some in hives exposed to the sun because they took flight sooner than we thought of watching them. We need never fear to shade a hive, since Virgil recommends it. If the roof does not project sufficiently to protect the hive from the sun in the heat of the day we would advise rough matting or any other temporary covering to be thrown over them. The most favourable aspect is towards the point where the sun is from ten o'clock till mid-day. They should never be turned to the east, and especially not to the north, where the cold and tempestuous winds greatly injure them.

Hives should not be placed high—on a first or second-floor, as we have sometimes seen them—unless they be completely sheltered, because the wind is less powerful near the ground, and therefore the bees are safer in less elevated situations.

We had some nine hives for several seasons out at a

SITUATION OF THE APIARY.

cottage in a deep valley sheltered on every side, and the hives were in a garden, covered over with very tall fruit trees. These did well every season; we had swarms for sale always early in May, and the honey harvest was very abundant. We attribute it all to the sheltered position of the hives; for example, not a single bee would be destroyed by the winds during the whole season, whilst the losses described at the head of this paper befel another apiary we had at the same time fully exposed. In the latter we never had swarms until July, and the honey was not worth the trouble of taking. We strongly urge every bee-farmer to make sure of this point at the beginning. If he wishes to be successful he must screen and shelter every hive.

Our Rustic Bee-shed will remove much of the difficulty. It keeps the hives in the shade during the whole of the working hours.

Note: the following results have been arrived at by most careful experiments: Bees fed with different kinds of sugar produce wax sooner and in greater abundance than those fed with pure honey. A pound of refined or lump sugar reduced to syrup produced 10 dr. 52 gr. of wax, of course much darker than that extracted from honey. An equal weight of dark-brown sugar produced 22 dr. 2¾ oz. of very white wax, or nearly one-sixth of the entire weight.

Mark the above result. It is cheaper and more economical to feed them with common brown sugar than even the best white lump sugar, because the brown makes more wax, and finer in quality.

By this method of bee-management, condemned stocks are useful and should not be despised. In the month of September I regularly visit all our cottage apiaries, and obtain the promise of all their condemned stocks. I have, in one instance, placed seven stocks in one hive; this afterwards made a profitable and most valuable colony. When I first commenced working up our condemned stocks I was laughed at by some of our intelligent bee-masters, for the simple reason that they could not understand or believe they could make sufficient comb for storing food for winter use. I do not advise anyone to commence building up colonies from single stocks; in such a case I do not wonder at numerous failures, simply because there are not sufficient bees to raise the heat necessary for wax-making or enough wax-workers to carry on the operation successfully. My advice to all is, never try to build up a stock at this late season with less than three stocks in each hive. Do not all or nearly all the workers die by the following April? I believe they do. Then is it not folly to place so many together? No, I reply, for, by the time named, the queen has got a good start for the season; if she is young and vigorous the workers will have prepared cells perhaps more in number than she can fill. If the colony is weak in the autumn it will never do any good; destroy it, or add it to some other stock.

THE BEE-STING.

Most bee-keepers will confess, that when they first began apiculture they had a dread of the bee-sting. We cannot, therefore, wonder that strangers, who have had no practical acquaintance with bees, should dread it; indeed, we believe this has been the greatest hindrance to apiculture, and is the chief cause why where we now only find one hive hundreds are not kept.

Bees, if injured, will sting their master, although he may have for years tended the hive, and become thoroughly acquainted with them; but it is seldom their anger is roused, excepting only under very trying circumstances. First let us learn how they may be excited so as to become really savage, and sting anyone who may be within reach, then how they may be rendered harmless, so as to be handled with impunity.

THE BEE-STING.

Bees when alone, or at some distance from their hives, will always try to evade man instead of attacking him; but when bees are gathered in a large colony, many thousands strong, they will then attack every intruder who ventures to disturb their homes. The worker bees, of which the hive is principally composed, are the soldiers and defenders of the colony, over which the queen reigns without a rival. The drones, or male bees, have no defensive weapons, only the workers are armed with stings. It may, however, be relied upon as a rule, that the worker bee *will not sting except in its own defence*. The point of the sting is barbed like an arrow. When the bee makes use of the sting it is generally driven so deep, especially in a fleshy substance, as not again to be easily withdrawn. In losing her sting she parts with a part of the intestines, and, of necessity, must soon die. We cannot, therefore, suppose she will even make use of the sting except when threatened itself with death, or when she is excessively irritated. Under certain circumstances they become quite ferocious, and cannot be pacified for several days; such is the case when they are being robbed by bees from other hives; or, worse still, by the subtle and sly wasp. Nor will they tolerate a sweating horse, or anything that has a disagreeable smell. The apiarian should not disturb his hives, or attempt to perform any operation amongst the bees when he perspires, and, if he is wise, he will exclude all perfumes from his toilet. Huber clearly shows that bees have an acute sense of smell, but he appears to think it is only unpleasant odours that are offensive.

Bees dislike anything uncleanly : this may arise in part from their clean habits. It also irritates them to come upon them suddenly, or to pass the bee house in haste, swinging the arms about. The bee-master must go amongst his stocks calmly, and with great coolness. Breathing upon them will not be tolerated; and when a bee hums about your face never attempt to strike it, for if you do so a companion will soon be found to take up the quarrel, until in a short time you will be surrounded with an angry buzz. We have invariably found, when you are thus attacked, it is better to leave the vicinity of the hives for a short time, and to hide in a bush, or, if there are no bushes close by, lie down with the face towards the ground, and cover the ears, &c. with both hands; in a few minutes the angry insects will retire to the hive.

An old bee-keeper, more than two centuries since, wrote as follows:—" If thou wilt have the favour of thy bees, that they sting thee not, thou must avoid such things as offend them ; thou must not be unchaste or uncleanly; for impurity and sluttiness (themselves being most chaste and neat) they utterly abhor. Thou must not come amongst them smelling of sweat, or having a stinking breath, caused either through eating of leeks, onions, garlic, and the like, or by any other means, the noisomeness whereof is connected with a cup of beer. Thou must not come puffing or blowing unto them, neither hastily stir among them, nor resolutely seem to defend thyself when they seem to threaten thee; but softly move thy hand before thy face, gently put them by; and lastly, thou must be no stranger to them. In a word, thou must be chaste, cleanly, sweet, sober, quiet, and familiar; so will they love thee and know thee from all others. When nothing hath angered them, one may safely walk along by them; but if he stand still before them in the heat of the day, it is a marvel but one or other spying him will have a cast at him." The question now arises—If bees are so vicious, how must I work amongst them? Well, we think the following rule may be relied upon. Bees when terrified will immediately fill themselves with honey from the comb; when the honey bag is filled they become quiet and harmless. When bees are swarming it is generally

THE BEE-STING.

believed, and perhaps with some truth, that the bees being so intent upon removing with the queen to a new abode forget to sting—it is not that they forget to use their stings, but just before swarming they fill themselves with food (honey), therefore they are peaceable. Just so in respect to every operation performed by the skilful and experienced bee-farmer upon his stocks: he first terrifies them, then the after-work is easy. If, instead of first smoking or terrifying them, the hive is suddenly turned up to the light, the bees are so enraged and furious, that, if they are afterwards conquered, it is at the sacrifice of hundreds of the bees.

Some few years ago, an old man—evidently very poor, but one of that large class of persons who live on their wits—visited the village on purpose apparently to benefit the bee-keepers. He first made extensive inquiries from everybody he could get into conversation with as to the names of the bee-keepers, the number of hives to be found in their gardens, their position in society—in fact, nothing came amiss in the shape of information, then he laid his plan so as to visit the whole on one day.

He introduced himself as a well-known apiarian, but now, through misfortune, considerably reduced in his circumstances; then he told us of his wondrous success as a British bee-farmer, having kept as many as fifty hives at one time. Then he stated he had a secret how to manage them, worth untold wealth; and by its means the most timid person could work them without fear of being stung. This, of course, raised the curiosity of many, and they were determined to acquire this secret of successful management.

To cut short our tale, he asked those who were reputed well-to-do half a guinea for his secret, but cottagers, or farm-labourers, he only charged five shillings; when he had secured the money, then he, without a smile, told them to smoke the hive, before commencing operations, with *old fustian*.

After all, although the story may raise a smile, the old man's secret is of value; of course, anything causing sufficient smoke will answer equally well, but we are not aware of any material so handy, and at the same time so effective, as fustian.

This is the grand secret of quieting bees, and rendering them so amiable and good humoured that you may do almost anything with them—*first smoke them*.

The method to be pursued is simply this: procure a little tinder, or an old cotton stocking; ignite it so as to cause it to smoke plentifully; then cautiously proceed to the entrance or mouth of the hive, and for about a minute blow the smoke into the hive amongst the bees. At the first puff of smoke a peculiar hum is distinctly heard, which indicates that the bees are rushing to the top of the combs (where the honey is stored), where they suck up as much honey as their stomachs will contain. After this, turn up the hives, or, if they are Woodbury bar-frame hives, open the top board and take out bar after bar, filled with comb, and covered with thousands of the inmates, without fear of being stung—the bees appear powerless and quite bewildered, clinging to the comb. Some few may take to the wing and fly about—these, however, are generally peaceable.

In any case, no matter how much control the apiarian has over his stocks, we recommend him to wear a bee-dress. There are always a few bees in every hive very difficult to pacify; bees, perhaps, of bilious temperament, which cannot be charmed with smoke, and the momoment you approach the stand they will set up a peculiar piping hum (once heard, not easily mistaken) and dart without warning at your eyes. As it is not pleasant to have these useful organs swollen so as to be unable to see, we use on every occasion, excepting perhaps when hiving swarms, a bee-veil. They are very cheap, and should be in constant readiness. We make ours by doubling up a yard of black-leno muslin, and sewing up the two sides, leaving the bottom only open, like a plain bag. This is merely slipped over the hat, so as to cover completely the whole of the head and neck, then the coat is buttoned over it up to the chin, if possible; the brim of the hat holds it a sufficient distance from the face, &c. Thus shielded, no one need have the slightest alarm, but pull out the bars of the hive, covered over with hundreds of the bees, fearlessly; in fact, this simple protection gives courage to the most timid bee-farmer. Never use gloves of any kind, they are only in the way, and prevent free use of the fingers, which are needful in all apiarian operations.

Having given directions how to render the stocks harmless, we come now to another point—" taming the bees." " To tame vicious bees," says a writer in the *Scottish Gardener*, " we have only to accustom them to the form of human beings. A scarecrow, or what our Scotch friends call a bogle, placed in front of the hives is a great help. It can be shifted now and then, and to provoke a general attack, place a loose waving rag or handkerchief in the palm of the bogle. Bees attack the waving provoking handkerchief, and sting at it until their vice leaves them. That which scares crows tends to domesticate bees. If kept in a garden where men wander and children are often seen, and where they are not disturbed, bees are as tame and as peaceable as cocks and hens." Daniel Wildman made himself famous in the year 1766, in the West of England, for his command over bees. He often exhibited his bees before the nobility, as the following advertisement, which appeared in a London paper in 1772, will show:—
" June 20th, 1772.—Exhibition of bees on horseback, at

the Jubilee Gardens, Islington, this and every evening until further notice. The celebrated Daniel Wildman will exhibit several new and amazing experiments, never attempted before by any man in this or any other kingdom. The rider standing upright, one foot on the saddle, and one on the neck, with a mask of bees on his head and face. He also rides standing upright on the saddle, with the briddle in his mouth; and by firing a pistol, makes one part of the bees march over the table, and the other swarm in the air and return to their hive again, with other performances too tedious to insert. Admittance, Box and Gallery, 2s.; the other seats 1s." Another man has recently appeared as a bee-tamer at Saratoga, in America; it appears, however, that the poor fellow met with nothing but misfortune. We suspect the secret of Wildman's success was in his command over the queen bee.

REMEDIES FOR THE BEE-STING.

There have been published almost as many cures for the bee-sting as there are British Apiarians. It is questionable, however, if many of them are really efficacious.

When the honey-bee sends his barbed weapon through the skin and into the flesh of the human subject, it presses back upon two small bags which are filled with a poison. The venom is instantly ejected up a very fine tube into the flesh. The sting of the bee is formed exactly upon the same principle as the nettle sting. In both cases the finely-polished sting is hollow from the point or tip to the base, where it joins the bag. Again, in both instances, by direct pressure upon the bag, the poison is pushed up the hollow tube into the wound made to receive it. Immediately the venom comes into contact with the flesh a strange sensation is felt over the whole body, accompanied often with cold trembling of the limbs, and a fearful smarting pain where the sting has been inserted, a pain similar to that caused by the bite of the cobra. In a few moments the poison is taken up, and circulated with the blood over the whole system, although the smarting and swelling are experienced only in the place or part where the wound has been made; this is easily perceived by the flesh being slightly raised, like a small wart, and very white, showing that some deadly poison is at work. On each side of the sting, from the point downwards, are four small barbs or teeth, resembling, when seen beneath the microscope, the edge of a fine saw. The bee-sting differs from that of the wasp and hornet in this particular: the wasp, having no barbs, or much smaller ones, can sting frequently without either injuring itself or losing its sting; not so the honey-bee. In ninety-nine cases out of every hundred it loses its sting, and with it a part of the intestines, which naturally results in its death. Archdeacon Paley, in his *Natural Theology*, gives a good description of the bee-sting: "The action of the sting affords an example of the union of chemistry and mechanism: of chemistry in respect to the venom which can produce such fearful effects; of mechanism, as the sting is a compound instrument. The machinery would have been comparatively useless had it not been for the chemical process by which, in the insect's body, honey is converted into poison; and, on the other hand, the poison would have been ineffectual without an instrument to wound, and a syringe to inject it. Upon examining the edge of a very keen razor by the microscope, it appears as broad as the back of a pretty thick knife: rough, uneven, and full of notches and furrows, and so far from anything like sharpness, that an instrument as blunt as this seemed to be would not serve even to cleave wood. An exceedingly small needle being also examined, it resembled a rough iron bar out of a smith's forge. The sting of a bee, viewed through the same instrument, showed everywhere a polish amazingly beautiful, without the least flaw, blemish, or inequality, and ended in a point too fine to be discerned."

Frequently the effects of the sting in persons who are susceptible, and with tender skins, are felt for many days; and if the swollen part is irritated, or rubbed at the end of that period, the pain is again slightly felt. But it may be a slight satisfaction to such persons to know that the effect of the venom is not so violent in after-years—certainly, the sickly sensation, accompanied with the smarting pain, is not regarded with so much horror after being felt several times. Much, also, depends upon the state of the body at the time: if the skin is in a state of perspiration, or the body at a high temperature, or the person is ailing with any disease, the effects are much more violent.

When stung, the first thing to be attended to is the removal of the sting from the flesh; for, if left to itself, it sinks deeper and deeper, all the time ejecting more and more of the venom; but if the sting is immediately removed very little poison can have been injected beneath the skin. It is easy to tender advice, but often difficult to follow it. The next thing to be attended to is not to rub or irritate the part. If violently rubbed it puts the blood in active circulation, and so the poison taken up in the circulation is rapidly disseminated.

One of the remedies which has lately appeared in the newspapers—although it is very old—is to apply damp soil (earth) to the wound; this is said to act like a charm, and to take away immediately the pain and inflammation. The real fact is, anything cold applied has a soothing influence for a limited period, such as cold water. This is also strongly recommended by many bee-keepers. Langstroth,

REMEDIES FOR THE BEE-STING.

the great American bee-keeper, speaks highly in its favour for its mollifying effects; he thinks it dissolves the poison and checks at once the after inflammation. I have applied it direct from the pump when severely stung on the wrist and arm, but I cannot say that it had more than a temporary effect.

The venom being of a strong acid nature, any alkali which will counteract it is useful as a remedy. On this ground many persons apply liquid ammonia, or hartshorn, but it should be applied with care. Liquor potassæ also is often used with beneficial results. In "Bee-keeping for the many" tobacco and its juice are recommended, to be applied as follows: "Take ordinary fine cut smoking or chewing tobacco, and lay a pinch of it in the hollow of your hand, and moisten it, and work it over until the juice appears quite dark coloured; then apply it to the part stung, rubbing in the juice with the tobacco between your thumb and fingers as with a sponge. As fast as the tobacco becomes dry, add a little moisture, and continue to rub and press out the juice upon the inflamed spot during five or ten minutes; and if applied soon after being stung it will cure in every case. Before I tried it I was frequently laid up with swollen eyes and limbs for days, now it is an amusement to get stung." Not having personally tested the tobacco remedy, I cannot vouch for its efficacy; yet it may, like the others, be of service if quickly applied.

Plaintain leaves (way-bread of Cheshire and Lancashire villagers) bruised and pressed on the wound are a reputed specific.

Longfellow, in the "Song of Hiawatha," mentions bees as preceding the white man, and soon after he settles the plantain also makes it appearance. It is a fact that the plantain follows invariably the steps of the European, and from this circumstance it is called by the Indians "White

Man's Foot." It seems strange that Longfellow should refer to it in the same stanza with bees, as though it were a remedy for the bee venom—

> "Wheresoe'er they move, before them
> Swarms the stinging fly the Ahmo,
> Swarms the bee the honey-maker;
> Whereso'er they tread, beneath them
> Springs a flower unknown among us,
> Springs the White Man's Foot in blossom."

The juice of the poppy allays the pain; this acts solely as a sedative. Laudanum prepared from poppies will act much more speedily, still the swelling or inflammation will not be arrested with its after effect. Mr. Wagner, a German apiarian, states he always applies the juice from ripe honeysuckle berries, and has never known it to fail as a remedy.

Every bee-keeper has his special and never-failing cure, and I have mine, which I now for the first time make public. A few summers ago when staying in Shropshire, one Sabbath afternoon, passing through a quiet village, I saw what to me was a joyous sight. In a cottage garden, under the care of an aged widow, I was gratified by seeing arranged in two rows not less than forty strong stocks of bees. As I was looking over the hives, without interfering with them, a bee, perhaps previously angered by some cause, without any warning stung me just beneath the right eye. The poor widow at once went into her cottage, and, bringing out her hair-oil bottle, began to rub the oil gently into the wound, with the happiest result; in fact, I was overjoyed to feel the pain almost instantly cease, and the part was not afterwards at all inflamed or swollen, though at first the sting had a dreadful effect upon me, the swelling and smarting being frightful. Ever since this well-remembered Sabbath, I have, when stung, without loss of time removed the sting and applied *plain olive oil*, rubbing it gently into the part, then a small quantity of *tincture of arnica*, and, although I have since been stung hundreds of times, I have not in a single instance after applying the above experienced the slightest inconvenience; so that a bee-sting to me is a matter of no moment, for the part, although very painful for a few seconds, never inflames; the pain disappears as if by magic, and not the slightest swelling is perceived.

Some persons when stung faint, and lose all command of themselves: in such cases it is well to have at hand, so that it can be used without loss of time, a small quantity of sal volatile, of which a teaspoonful should be taken internally in a tablespoonful of cold water; this will speedily remove the faintness. I have known an apiarian do nothing when stung but suck the part with his mouth, if on the hands; but he suffered much from headaches and loss of appetite, which I attributed to the venom. The place bitten by a serpent may be sucked with impunity, without any evil results. It thus differs widely from the bee venom, which, whilst acting powerfully upon the blood, will also vitiate the stomach. It will be well to bear this in memory.

THE SWARMING SEASON.

No part of the bee-keeper's year is so much prized as the swarming season, which ranges in England from May to July. It is also an anxious period, on account of there being no certainty as to the exact time when a swarm will issue from the parent hive. We have known many young bee-farmers who lost much valuable time from being constantly on the watch, from fear lest they should lose a stock by not being on the spot when they left.

Although there may be much uncertainty about the particular day when a swarm will venture forth, there can be none as to the part of the day when it issues. It is true we have had swarms from 7 A.M. to 7 P.M., but we never knew a first swarm later than 12 A.M. The first swarm is led by the old reigning queen, and she has got too old a head on her shoulders either to emigrate when rain is falling, or in the after part of the day, when she may have but little time to select a favourable spot for her future home—*i.e.* if the place which may have been selected by the scouts is unsuitable. She also takes good care to choose a fine and warm morning. So far as the second swarm is concerned, we may judge almost to a day when a swarm will leave by the peculiar piping of her majesty.

The first is only rightly named "swarm," the second is called a "cast," and the third is often nicknamed a "colt," whilst a fourth, by way of distinction from the third, is called a "filly." A swarm from a swarm is justly named a "maiden swarm."

In many villages it is customary when swarming takes place to make a horrid noise with tin cans, kettles, or ringing with a key on a frying-pan. Sometimes this is carried to great lengths. It is not unusual to observe some half-dozen females, busy as possible, trying which can make the greatest noise. It is, however, scarcely needful to say that this is really unnecessary. If anything will bewilder the queen, who, to a certain extent, guides the swarm to the selected bough, it must be this intolerable uproar. We have for several years noted many apiarian customs with extreme care and jealousy in this matter. We have observed that the queen is not, in nineteen instances out of each twenty, lost, when the tanging is discarded; but in numerous cases of ringing we have known the swarm to return to the hive, showing us that the queen was either lost or had never left the hive. We have been unmercifully condemned as a heretic and unbeliever by all the good old maiden ladies of the village in which we reside merely because we have opposed this needless task of ringing the swarms, and would never allow it to be used in our garden. In everything else we can gain their goodwill, but here we have failed, so we are given to understand, by their constantly asserting "your bees cannot prosper."

We now stay to inquire why it was first introduced by our forefathers. Like many other customs, which at first were really useful, and originally valuable for their intended purpose, it has been corrupted, or become useless. In days long since past, when stones even were quite a sufficient guide as landmarks, and as such were honoured, bees then were far more valuable than now, because of their scarcity. Their owners, when swarming was perceived, at once gave timely notice to all the neighbourhood, by tanging or ringing, that the swarm was the right and property of the person so occupied in ringing. By thus giving notice he was allowed the privilege of following, or what we should now call trespassing, on his neighbour's land to claim his swarm. We also believe they had another object in view in thus giving notice, viz.: for the neighbours to come forward in a friendly way to aid him in securing the swarm. We are aware another reason has been assigned for this custom, which is nothing but pure superstition; it has been stated that the tanging was intended to drive away evil spirits, and prevent them having any influence over the bees.

Swarming is simply this,—the old hive becomes overpeopled by its industrious inmates, so, not having sufficient room for storing and breeding, they are compelled to emigrate. When the hive becomes thus overstocked, we observe them hanging out at the entrance in a large cluster, not unlike an immense bunch of grapes. This is the first sign of a prime or first swarm. We have known them under these circumstances, if it should fortunately happen that the bees observe a small opening in the floor-board sufficiently large for them to creep through, at once commence making combs beneath the stand, for bees do not like being idle—they make hay when the sun shines.

Many intelligent apiarians recommend the Nadiring system, especially for inexperienced bee-keepers. One author advises his readers to purchase a large quantity of American cheese-boxes, and, after making a slight opening in the lid, to place them beneath the hive; he intimates to all respectable labourers that by so doing they will make at the very least 100*l.* per annum. We knew one poor fellow so led away by this reasoning as to give up a good situation to attend to his bees, quieting his better half by assuring her he should make a good living by it; but the result in the autumn rather rudely shook his faith when he found himself a heavy loser. But this nadiring most certainly, if adopted in time and the bees take to the boxes, will stop swarming, but it is no advantage. Let us always set it down as a rule, that the nearer we manage our stocks so as to resemble the operations of Nature the more profitable it will be in the end; and Nature says bees never do so well as when we allow them to swarm.

AMERICAN SWARM SIGNAL.

The Americans have introduced a novelty called the "Swarm Signal," but it may be questionable whether this novelty will ever come into general use in our English apiaries, because in hundreds of cases it is not wanted, for the bee-stand is often either beneath the window or close by the door, when owned by cottagers, so that a swarm seldom makes its appearance without being speedily noticed

AMERICAN SWARM SIGNAL.

by one of the family. In other instances the gardener is never very far away at the time of day when swarming takes place. The annexed illustration will convey a more perfect idea of the instrument than any mere verbal description. It consists of a wire cage, F, about a foot in length; this, when placed over the mouth of the hive on the edge of the bottom-board, is firmly held by the weight E, resting upon a thin iron plate marked O, which is fastened to one corner of the cage; the signal K is attached to a string beneath the weight E. When fixing to the hive, just before a swarm is expected, it must be so placed

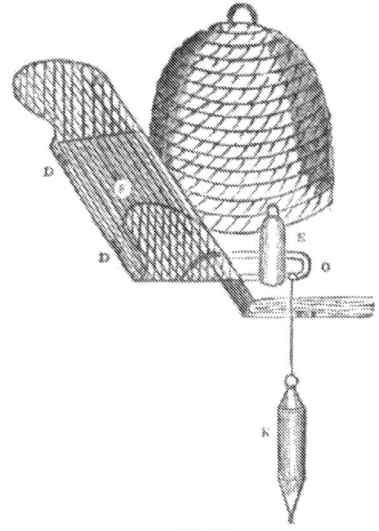

SWARM SIGNAL.

that only about three-fourths of the entrance is covered by the cage, thus not interfering with the workers; this can be managed by sliding the hive gently to the edge of the bottom or floor-board. On the sharp point of the signal K a gun-cap is fixed, and so hung that when freed by the weight it should drop on a brick placed beneath the signal on the ground; when the swarm is leaving the hive they crowd into the cage in their haste to escape, so that by the weight of the bees in the cage F the signal is liberated and falls on the brick, thus apprising the happy bee-master of his good fortune. Small holes are made in the cage at D D to allow the workers to escape, for it often happens, even before swarming, that many bees become prisoners. If the report made by the explosion of the gun-cap is not sufficiently loud to be heard, the signal should be bored and a small charge of gunpowder inserted to communicate with the cap.

HIVING SWARMS IN HIGH TREES.

One of the most difficult things in the experience of all young bee-keepers is run-away swarms, and swarms which seek the highest bough in any of the large apple or pear trees in the neighbouring garden. In the case of run-away swarms follow them if you can, but in reference to the swarms in a high bough this is not so difficult a task as may appear at first sight.

We watched with much interest a cottager's wife recently hiving a swarm up in an apple-bough; I tendered no advice, but simply watched all her operations, which were simple enough. She procured a common potato or half-measure hamper, and fastened it to the top of a long pike, then holding it beneath the swarm shook the bough as vigorously as possible under the circumstances, and brought her swarm down safely; they afterwards quietly entered the hive. This was a rough way of hiving. I hope none

HIVING SWARMS IN HIGH TREES.

of my readers will follow her example. I have used some time for this purpose a bag made with stiff black leno stitched. Around the mouth I attach a little very thick wire, to prevent it closing when being used; the bag is then fastened or nailed near the top of a long pole made of deal wood, about 9 feet in length and 2 inches in thickness, or like a clothes-prop, but at the summit, about 6 inches above the bag, I nail a bit of wood to prevent the pole from splitting, as well as to act as a hammer, to beat or shake the bough on which the swarm is settling. The

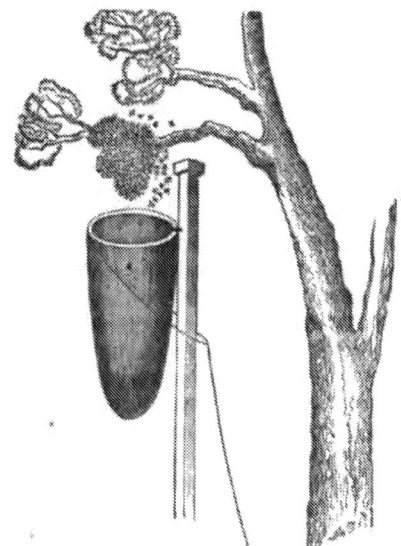

MODE OF SECURING A SWARM OF BEES.

above illustration will fully explain how to make and work the bag. To the wire ring, if desired—although it will act far better without—a string may be tied, and held in the hand of the operator, and, when the bees are shaken into the bag, by pulling the cord they are prevented from escaping.

We make use of it thus. Having got it in readiness, when the bees are observed to begin clustering, of course the first thing to be attended to is the hive and table on which they are to be placed for a few minutes after hiving before they are finally removed to their permanent stand. Then suddenly shake the bough with the end of the pole, the bees will drop into the bag—very few will be left on the branch after a vigorous shake. Slowly bringing them down to the table, hold the bag for a few minutes beside the hive, which should be slightly raised on the side nearest the bees, to allow of free ingress. The bees, seeing a home in readiness, will not be long in taking possession of the new tenement. You need not fear securing the queen at the first shake, and, if any of the bees are at all disposed to take refuge again on the bough, lay across it a smoking or smoldering rag, which will quickly drive away every bee to the hive below. The table should be placed beneath the tree if possible.

It will not take long to hive them in this easy way. I have succeeded in securing them, persuading them to settle in the new home, and removing them to the stand, in fifteen minutes; in half-an-hour afterwards they have commenced working as if nothing had happened. We first learned this simple plan from Quinby's *Bee Book*, but it seems still to be unknown by bee-keepers in this country.

ON FEEDING BEES.

We have not always sunshiny weather, clouds come and rain—rain coming down incessantly for days together. All seasons are not alike; some years are noted for their plentiful supply of honey. When we have good corn years, as a rule we have good honey harvests, and *vice versa*. There are many summers when the bees in stock-hives require little or no feeding, and, unfortunately, there are other years when they ought to be fed constantly. Again, some years—usually wet summers—are noted for their fine and abundant swarms and little honey. Being unable to go out for honey, the empty cells are filled with eggs by the queen, and large swarms are the result.

Feeding is but little practised by cottage bee-keepers. The prevailing notion appears to be that it is folly to feed your bees in summer. If they cannot find food in summer when can they?

It is also thought sinful to give any sugar or honey to early swarms; to feed them just when establishing a new colony is sure, people say, to make them idle. Nothing can be further from the truth; instead of causing them to be idle, it infuses new life and energy into them, and causes them to labour with greater earnestness. There are times when bees ought to be fed.

Do not under any circumstances neglect to feed your young swarms; and never forget there are such things in bee-culture as "hunger swarms." A swarm issues from the parent hive, and for many days afterwards we have nothing but dull, damp, and rainy weather keeping the bees indoors, so that they are unable to forage for themselves. In this case, except food is given to them, they must die. It is but seldom they leave the hive even under such distressing circumstances; or, if they quit their home, it is to go to another hive in the neighbourhood. A friend had a late swarm; it had been hived about a month, when one day he turned it up to see how they were going on inside. Judge his surprise to observe a large portion of them dead on the floor-board. He at once began to feed them with honey; in a few days the hum of peace and prosperity was again heard: thus he timely saved the stock from starvation. When a natural swarm leaves the parent hive, they carry away with them as much honey as will last them for food three days. The real object the bees have in view when they fill their honey-bags before swarming is to be able to begin building combs. The first day, if not the first hour, they are hived in an empty domicile, they lay the foundation of their new home. Bees can prepare more wax from a pound of sugar than from the same quantity of honey. It is therefore wise economy to give syrup to the recent swarms, and so enable them to gather honey, which they are only too willing to do, and store it in the cells they are rapidly making from the syrup.

Bees are not made idle by feeding them. Your bees will be idle if they are forced to stop in the hive through rainy weather, for which neither you nor they are responsible. Poor things, they are actually dying from want of food: give them a little syrup; how thankful they seem for your kindness, and show it too by working away at cell-building as fast as possible night and day. *No time is lost.* And how can they rear the brood without food? One of the most pitiable sights in bee-keeping is to see the stocks throwing out their young before they are mature, to perish. Most bee-keepers have seen in early autumn the young drones cast out: they are white and soft, called nymphs. They will not do this except compelled from lack of food; they love their young quite as much as do other creatures. Whatever you do, feed your helpless stocks when newly hived. Don't stint them, be liberal, and you will have in the end an abundant harvest.

In wet summers often lift up your hives, and if you find they are becoming lighter in weight, when they should be gaining day by day, don't blame your bees, but feed

ON FEEDING BEES.

them with sugar. It keeps up the bees, and induces both the queen to keep on breeding and workers to scour the country at every favourable opportunity in search of honey-dew. Never for a moment harbour the thought that because it is summer your bees require no attention: they need much more care in summer than in winter. It certainly is disheartening, and enough to make most persons give up the pursuit in disgust, when they see their stocks dwindling away in summer, when they ought to be paying interest for the capital invested in them the preceding year. The working man or farm labourer in such a case is to be pitied, but my chief object in penning these lines is to persuade him not to give up in despair: a great reward looms in the future; every summer cannot be bad and unprofitable, and the sun shines all the brighter after the storm.

The principal feeding time, however, is in the autumn (September and October). Those stocks which are to be kept on the bench during the winter, for next year's harvest, need much attention about this time. Some bee-keepers make it a practice to keep on feeding all the winter; this is the worst thing that can be done, and nothing that I know tends to weaken the stock so much as this system. All practical apiarians now strongly recommend all the stock hives to be weighed in the autumn, and those that do not contain at least twenty pounds of food (honey) should be immediately fed up to this point. Then they can settle down for the whole winter, without any other care or looking after, except perhaps to see that they are kept dry. But if the feeding is done by small driblets all the winter it causes robbing and fighting; worst of all, the bees coming out of the warm hives on the floor-board (for when fed in the winter by cottagers it is generally done on a plate, either outside, or just beneath the hive under the combs) are often paralyzed with the cold, and being unable to return to the combs, die.

The spring should not be neglected. The stocks in March are sometimes found destitute of honey. This is often the case after a mild winter, for it has repeatedly been noticed by apiarians, that whereas in severe cold, frosty winter very little honey, comparatively speaking, has been consumed, in a mild winter nearly all the honey has been eaten. How is it the bees in Siberia winter so well? We should naturally suppose they would be killed by the intense cold which prevails for four months in that bleak region. It is not so. The peasantry keep fine and strong colonies, and send to other nations many tons of pure honey. The Americans deposit their hives in ice houses all the winter: the stocks, instead of being weaker than if they wintered in the open air, come out all the stronger in the following spring, and have consumed far less honey. In cold weather the bees cluster closely together, and are to a certain degree dormant. In mild weather, on the contrary, they are very active. In this state, when not clustering for warmth, they must consume the honey to keep up their natural heat. From October to March an ordinary sized stock will eat fifteen pounds of honey. Dr. Bevan states, a stock will generally consume from October to March one to one-and-a-half pounds of honey per month. But from March to the end of May, when breeding is going on at a rapid rate, they consume double that quantity. If a cold May comes after a warm April it causes sad destruction in cottage apiaries. This may be prevented by feeding. All bee-farmers should feed heavily if the month of May should prove wet and cold; they will be well repaid. I have known fine stocks perish through want of feeding in spring after wintering well with very little loss. With timely attention and a little food in March they might have been saved. Spring feeding also causes the queen to deposit eggs in the cells, thus strengthening the stocks and causing early swarming.

ON FEEDING BEES.

The question often arises—How shall I feed my bees? and what kind of food will be the best and most profitable to use?

I have frequently been amused by the primitive utensils still in use for offering food to bees. The most common way of giving liquid food is in pieces of elder-wood. A straight stem of elder is cut out of the hedge, about the thickness of the thumb, and a slice cut off equally all the way down, so as to expose the pith. The pith is scooped out with the point of a penknife, and each end is stopped with a plug of wood; it is then ready for use. This bee-feeder has the recommendation of simplicity. It is also simple in use, for after filling it with honey, or sugar, it is thrust through the mouth of the hive. I distinctly recollect my parents feeding their bees by placing sugar on plates, then lifting up the hives and placing it beneath the combs. Many villagers have a large soup-plate, which is half filled with the food, and left exposed near the bee-bench. This way of feeding I must condemn as being worse than useless. The first summer I kept bees, one stock, being rather feeble, required much feeding. I tried the elder-trough, and placed it full of syrup beneath the hive; however, it taught me a lesson which I shall never forget. It had not been beneath the hive longer than an hour when I noticed a few robber bees from another apiary busy taking away the spoils; these, of course, soon returned home, and brought with them a large band, who commenced speedily a war of extermination with my weak stock. The battle for about three hours was the most fierce I have ever witnessed. The ground around the apiary was strewn with hundreds of dead and dying bees, and at one time the air was literally darkened with bees in my small garden. Fortunately for me, a heavy thunderstorm came on in the afternoon of the same day; this, together with the precaution of completely stopping up the entrance to my hive, saved the stock from actual extermination, but it never did me any good. A word to the intelligent cottager. Never feed your bees in the daytime, and never expose any food to attract robbers, who are only too plentiful when the honey harvest is over, or in the autumn.

Feeding should only be attempted at night; then there are no thieves abroad, and the bees if excited do not in the darkness attempt to leave the hive. In the daytime when food is given to the stock they become so excited that they wander about, or fly abroad in a state of confusion. Woe be to the housekeeper if she should be boiling her preserves just at this time. She will be astonished to find her kitchen full of bees. The door may be closed, barred, and bolted, too; every window and conceivable crevice closed as well. It is of no use, they will flock down the chimney—anywhere, to obtain the desired or coveted food—such is the effect of feeding in the daytime. Watch the robber as, daubed with honey, he alights at the entrance of his home: several of his companions speedily set to work cleaning his body and wings before he enters. No sooner does he enter, than quite an army hastily, as if time was too precious to be wasted, speed on their wings to follow the steps of their companion. In less than an hour from the time the first bee discovered the sweets hundreds will be on the spot. How they find out the exact spot I am unable to state; whether the discoverer after unloading his burden leads the way, or whether he can give them due information, it is impossible to say.

Let the bee-master make it a rule, if he wishes not to suffer loss by wars, never to feed his stocks except at night, nor to leave the food exposed. Dr. Cumming, the "Times Bee-Master," recommends a large plate filled with food to be placed somewhere near the apiary, open

ON FEEDING BEES.

to all the bees. This may do for the wealthy bee-master, who keeps bees solely for his amusement, but it will never answer for the cottager to feed all the bees within two or three miles around his apiary. Undoubtedly the best way to feed up the stocks in September is from the top of the hive. If my readers keep only the round-topped straw hives, a small hole or opening must be made in the crown; it is done without difficulty. Choose the middle of a fine warm day, when the bees are working hard; and with either a razor or a strong pocket-knife, the point of the blade very sharp, cut a circular hole in the centre, about three inches in diameter; very few bees will be disturbed, and unless the comb has been made within the past month it will not be injured. I have sometimes had great difficulty to persuade my bee-keeping friends to adopt this method, because they thought the combs would fall, and thus ruin the whole hive. The bees take good care to secure their combs, not only at the top where they commence to build, but all down the sides as well. Not the slightest fear need be entertained on this point. When you have cut the straw out, trim the sides from the bits of straw that hang loosely round the opening, thus saving your bees the trouble of completing your work. Preserve with care the round piece of straw that you have cut out: it will be useful to put in the place again when you have finished feeding.

You are sure in removing plates, &c. from beneath the hive to kill many of your bees, besides enticing vagrants and robbers. Never nourish your bees from beneath; all wickedness and evil come from below, so in bee-hives; every good comes down from above, so in bee-hives, and your little singing happy inmates know it too, without tapping on the skep and speaking to them; therefore encourage them to look for all good to come down from above, they will not forget it as long as they live. There are two excellent ways of feeding at the top of the hive. One of these ways is by the Lancashire bee-feeder; it is a simply constructed appliance, made of tin, zinc, wood, or earthenware. I prefer the latter. Bee-masters seldom wash and keep scrupulously clean the bee requisites. It is better, if this be so, to use the earthenware feeder, because this will of itself be sweet. Wood especially, and often tin and zinc, are apt to turn the food sour, which causes dysentery and death.

LANCASHIRE BEE-FEEDER.

The wood-cut represents the Lancashire bee-feeder. It is made usually of tin, and will hold about six pounds of syrup; it is 9 inches in diameter, as sold in the Manchester seed-stores. When filled with the food, it is covered with a tin lid, which fits closely. I prefer it when covered with glass, because you can then watch the bees taking up the food, and can more easily ascertain when it is empty. After filling with syrup place it on the hive, with the circular opening seen in the illustration over the hole you have made in the crown of the hive. The entrance is through the centre of the feeder. Both the inside and the outside of the entrance are lined with perforated zinc, so as to present a rough surface for the bees to climb, and the top of the entrance tube is half-an-inch lower than the sides of the feeder, so that when covered with its lid it will allow the bees to climb over to the wood float, which rests on the surface of the syrup, and sinks as the bees take it to store it in the hive. With this feeder I have given a starving stock as much as six pounds of syrup in the course of one night. When the feeder is first given to the hive, it is well to smear the entrance-tube with honey, and to drop a little through the hole into the hive amongst the bees; this will at once attract them, and cause them to ascend quickly into the feeder.

The float is made of very thin wood, covered with small holes made with a red-hot wire (an awl or gimlet would split the wood), through which the bees suck their food without injury. In many feeders hundreds of bees are actually drowned; this cannot occur with the Lancashire feeder. Another feeder on the same principle is advertised by Pettitt, of Dover. It is made of wood, and will hold four pounds of liquid food.

A cheap way of feeding is this: directly the hole is cut in the crown of the hive, lay on it a piece of perforated zinc, 4 inches square, to cover the opening and prevent any bees from coming through, because when bees are excited with feeding they are apt to overlook the kindness, and to sting even their master if he interferes too much. A pickle-bottle, or a bottle of any kind with a wide mouth, may form your bee-feeder. Fill it with liquid food, and tie over its mouth a bit of black net, leno, or coarse muslin. Invert the bottle upon the perforated zinc, and steady it with a bit of wood on each side, to prevent it falling, and the bees will suck up the food through the small holes in the zinc. This is a very handy plan, and is nearly always employed by apiarians who use the Woodbury-hives. It has many advantages, especially in cold weather. The bees are not chilled in procuring the food, for they are kept within the hives.

Several substitutes for honey have been recommended as food for bees. Many apiarians who can afford it, however, still prefer honey when feeding up weak colonies in the autumn, because, say they, it prevents "dysentery," of which disease many bees die in early spring. Dysentery is caused often from eating sour food. If liquid food turns sour in the cells, it may prove injurious, but this seldom happens.

Amongst the substitutes may be mentioned sugar, lump and raw, sugar-candy, and barley-sugar. The

"Times" Bee-Master strongly urges bee-keepers to use nothing but sugar mixed with beer; if anything is liable to sour this is, and I would not recommend anyone to use beer-food. Langstroth states he has for several years used West Indian honey. To remove its impurities, and prevent it from either souring or candying in the cells, it should have a little water added to it, then be boiled for a few minutes, and set to cool; the scum on the top should then be removed. He also mixes three pounds of honey, two of brown sugar, and one pound of water. The latter would be both an excellent and cheap food.

The Rev. M. Kleine says in the *Bienenzeitung*, "The use of sugar-candy for feeding bees gives to bee-keeping a security which it did not possess before. Still, we must not base over-sanguine expectations on it, or attempt to winter very weak stocks, which a prudent apiarian should at once unite with a stronger colony. I have used sugar-candy for feeding for the last five years, and made many experiments with it, which satisfy me that it cannot be too strongly recommended, especially after unfavourable summers. It is prepared by dissolving two pounds of candy in a quart of water and evaporating by boiling about two gills of the solution, then skimming and straining through a hair sieve. Three quarts of this solution fed in autumn will carry a colony safely through the winter in an ordinary season."

Grape sugar for correcting sour wines is now extensively made from potato starch in various places on the Rhine, and has been highly recommended for bee-food. It can be obtained at a much lower price than cane sugar, and is better adapted to the constitution of the bee, as it contains the saccharine matter of honey, and hence is frequently termed honey-sugar.

It may be used either diluted with boiling water, or in its raw state, moist, as it comes from the factory. In the latter condition bees consume it slowly, and, as there is not the waste that occurs when candy is fed, I think it is better winter food.

The Rev. M. Sholz, of Silesia, recommends the following as a substitute for sugar-candy in feeding bees: Take one pound of honey and four pounds of pounded lump-sugar; heat the honey without adding water, and mix it with the sugar, working it together to a stiff doughy mass. When it is thoroughly incorporated cut it into slices, or form it into cakes or lumps, and wrap them in a piece of coarse linen, and place them in the frames. Thin slices enclosed in linen may be pushed down between the combs. The plasticity of the mass enables the apiarian to apply the food in any manner he may desire. The bees have less difficulty in appropriating this kind of food than where candy is used, and there is no waste.

By sliding a few sticks of candy under the frames or between the combs, a small colony may be fed in warm weather, without tempting robbers by the smell of liquid food. Langstroth gives the annexed recipe for making candy as bee-food:—

"Add water to the sugar, and clarify the syrup with eggs. Put about a teaspoonful of cream of tartar to about twenty pounds of sugar, and boil until the water is evaporated. To know when it is done dip your finger first into cold water and then into the syrup. If what adheres is brittle when chewed it is boiled enough. Pour it into shallow pans slightly greased, and, when cold, break it into pieces of a suitable size. After boiling, balm or any other flavour agreeable to the bees may be put into the syrup."

Some prefer barley-sugar to all other food for their bees. One cause for this is, the ease with which it can be given, and the certainty of the bees not being without food during winter so long as the barley-sugar can be seen unused on the floor-board. Not having employed it, we cannot speak personally as to its value ; but we give the following extract from *Bee-Keeping for the Many* :—

"By giving bees food in a solid state very great trouble and inconvenience will be avoided, both to the bees and to their proprietors ; for the former will be in no danger of drowning, and will also have a supply of food that they appear to like better than any that has ever before been given them; whilst the latter will be spared the trouble of preparing those compounds usually recommended, many of which I have always considered to be very injurious to the bees, and more especially so when given in large quantities in the autumn. After many experiments it is found that of all solids barley-sugar has the decided preference with the bees. They will take it before anything else that is offered to them, and the rapidity with which they dissolve it is quite surprising. It may be given either at the top of the hive where there is an opening, by tying half-a-dozen sticks together and covering them with a box or small hive, or even with a flower pot, or at the bottom, as in the common straw hive, by pushing a few sticks in at the entrance, for, unlike liquid food, it does not attract robbers nor cause fighting, although given in the daytime. It is certainly most convenient to be able to push a few sticks of barley-sugar under a weak hive, and to know that by so doing they are made secure from want for a time. The idea of expense may be a consideration with some persons, but it will be found that barley-sugar may be purchased for less than a shilling a pound, and it may be made for sixpence."

HOW TO PREPARE BARLEY-SUGAR FOR BEE-FEEDING.

Put two pounds of loaf sugar into a saucepan of water, and two spoonfuls of best vinegar ; put it on a gentle fire, let it boil for about twenty minutes, till the syrup becomes so thick that the handle of a spoon being dipped into it and then plunged into cold water, the syrup upon the handle is found quite crisp; when this is the case it is sufficiently boiled. Having an earthen dish or marble slab in readiness, well buttered, pour the syrup upon it, and when sufficiently cool to handle, clip it with scissors into strips the size desired.

Candy, barley-sugar, and other nice things may be employed, but I prefer plain loaf or lump sugar. This will in the end be found the cheapest food, besides the many advantages it possesses over most other foods: for example, if properly prepared it will not candy and become hard, or crystallized, therefore (except with water) unusable by the bees in the hives, nor do I believe it will turn sour. Some bee-masters think that when mint, lemon, &c., are added to the syrup, it is liked better by the bees; this, however, has lately been satisfactorily proved by careful experiment to be fallacious. The bees prefer the plain syrup without any flavouring ingredients. And when flavoured it is apt to entice robber bees, and cause serious fighting, whereas when given plain it is inodorous, and other stocks are unable to tell when feeding is going on.

I purchase only lump sugar, and boil three pounds of sugar with two pounds of water, for two or three minutes; when cold it is ready for use. Not a few bee-keepers add to the above syrup a small quantity of honey, just to flavour it, and cause the bees to take it up with greater readiness; this is simply a matter of choice. I never use honey. Honey, if good, can be sold for 1*s*. 6*d*. per pound. Syrup made as above costs only three pence a pound, supposing sugar is five pence each pound. This is a great saving; bees do well upon it, make whiter wax with it, and for every purpose pure syrup is equal to honey for feeding your stocks.

BEE-PASTURES.

All districts are not equally profitable for bee-keeping; but, except in the neighbourhood of chemical works, we have seldom known any open country downs or heaths which were not good honey districts. Can a district be overstocked with bees? If we had thought this at all possible we should not have written a work on *Bee-Farming*, for it is easy to be a bee-keeper,—keeping a single hive of bees in the cottage garden. But a *Bee-Farmer* is one who, thoroughly understanding his business, has, by dint of careful attention, raised his thirty, forty, or fifty stocks.

This is the case in America. In some of the States, in the yearly agricultural return to the Government, a part of the form is specially assigned for a return of the number of hives, and probable yield per hive. Thus the importance of bee-farming is becoming every year more and more recognised. We trust the day is not far distant when it will be so in the British Islands.

Mr. Pettigrew says on this subject, "If a twenty-acre field of grass, well sprinkled with the flowers of the white clover, yield to the suck of bees 100 lbs. at least per day, value 5*l.*, and twenty acres of good heather yield probably 200 lbs. of honey every day, value 20*l.*, who will venture to calculate and give the sum total of honey value of all the counties of Great Britain and Ireland? . . Who can accurately weigh or number the millions upon millions of pounds of honey that pass away (ungathered by bees) into the atmosphere? Who can estimate the millions of pounds' worth of honey thus wasted on the 'desert air?'

"Suppose a mild form of *mania* were to seize the railway porters of the stations of the various railway companies of this country; and suppose it were to run in the direction of bee-hives. Well, what then? There can be no better position for bees than the banks of our railways. If fifteen hives were placed on an average per mile, how much income would be derived? At the rate of only 1*l.* per hive annually (about one-half the usual rate) 500 miles would return 7,500*l.* yearly. If our worthy porters were to receive Christmas presents to the tune of 15*l.* per mile of line, they would doubtless be pleased and full of gratitude —'A land flowing with milk and honey in this England of ours.'"

In Cheshire we have observed good honey yield is obtained from lime and sycamore trees. What more interesting sound than the cheerful hum of the honey bee in the early season, as we stand beneath the shade of a large lime-grove?

We must not suppose that bees gather all their rich stores from the garden. If they were to depend upon the supply from cultivated flowers we should have but little honey. The chief sources of honey in this country are the white or Dutch clover and the heather; the buckwheat yields a large quantity, but it is not cultivated so extensively as to make the supply good. The honey gathered from the heather is dark-coloured, but of a rich wild flavour; this is principally collected in the autumn. Our stocks are now known to have the finest honey in April and May; this is more pure and better flavoured than any other, and is procured from the clover. Bees kept on open downs, or in the neighbourhood of extensive pasture lands, always pay the best in a pecuniary point of view; they feed principally on the clover. We spoke recently to a poor widow who gains the best part of her living from bee-keeping—nay, it is her great boast that she has never troubled the parish for a penny, but her bees have been a sure source of income. When we have heard nothing in other quarters but complaints about the wretched honey-harvest, she can often glean about 40 lbs. of rich white honey from each stock. So we asked her opinion as to where her bees pastured. Her reply was quite characteristic; pointing to the long level stretch of sheep lands lying before us, she said, "Ah! if I kept a cow, I could not even be allowed to turn her in the lanes, and if I allowed her to stray in the fields I should be fined, but they cannot fine my bees, and these can pasture upon all the duke's lands."

We have known a single hive gain as much as 10 lbs. of honey per day from the clover blossoms.

The heather has been highly extolled as a rich honey-yielding plant, in fact, hundreds of hives are taken to the moors in the autumn by Lancashire cotton operatives; these are brought home sometimes exceedingly heavy; but we prefer the clover honey.

To mention all the honey-yielding plants would take up too much space, though some are preferable to others, such are the wallflower, mignonette, some of the old fashioned roses, the fruit-trees, &c. The borage, mustard, and raspberry are also excellent honey plants, still, being limited in cultivation, the supply of honey from them is uncertain.

The famed Narbonne honey is said to be collected from the wild rosemary, which is as abundant on the hills of the South of France as the wild thyme is in England.

Honey-dew—a sticky exudation of the aphis—found on the upper surface of leaves on lime and other trees, is often collected in large quantities by our bees, but we cannot trace any difference produced by it in the honey, perhaps because it is largely mixed with honey gathered from flowers.

Honey harvests are not equally good or large in all years. As a rule wet summers are the least productive of honey, but the best for swarms. Every fourth or fifth year we observe an enormous yield of honey: it is wise to be in readiness to take advantage of it when it does come round. Which is the best honey season, a wet or a dry one? A long drought soon destroys the harvest of honey, and a too wet season is even worse; a medium betwixt the two is, we find, the best. We base this upon the past ten years' experience. When we hear fears expressed about an expected drought, the bees are then storing honey rapidly if this happens to be in early summer, but if it continues the honey gradually becomes scarce. A tolerably moist season is after all the best, for the secretion of the honey depends much upon the state of the atmosphere. During dry easterly winds the fields present to the bees nothing but barrenness, and if they have no stores to fall back upon they begin to starve, which is soon discovered by their casting out the brood. When the weather is moist and sultry, and the air charged with electricity, honey is most abundant. The bees know this only too well, for, instead of idling at home, singing "a better day is coming on," they work to make hay while the sun shines. Huber remarks that the collection is never more abundant, nor their operations in wax more active, than when the wind is in the south, the air moist and warm, and a storm approaching. Heat too long protracted, cold rains, and a north wind, entirely stop honey gathering.

How far bees will go in search of honey is a question on which we scarcely venture to give an opinion, we believe, however, the average distance will be found not to exceed two miles, which would cover a circular area of nearly thirteen square miles, taking the hive as a centre. This opinion is shared by most thoughtful apiarians. We have seen our Ligurians about two miles from their hive, at a time when no other Italian bees were kept in the district, so we think this evidence may be relied upon, but it is the only test by which we ever tried them.

As to the profit of keeping bees, Wallace states that the pasturage of the United Kingdom is sufficient to produce 12,000,000 pounds of honey and 3,000,000 pounds of wax annually: the income derived from this, calculating the honey at 1*s*. 6*d*. per pound, and the wax at 2*s*. per pound, is 1,200,000*l*. Bearing in mind the very moderate cost or outlay in keeping the bees to secure this immense revenue, it is really a question of no small importance, not only to the well-to-do farmer, but to the humble labourer and cottager, if there is not here opened out a very fair prospect of assistance in gaining daily bread.

The same writer supposes a person to start with two hives, which he calculates at 3*l*. 10*s*. (of course they may be purchased for less than half that amount); allowing the hives to double their number annually, they would increase to such an extent that at the tenth year 1,024 hives would be the result, which, taking their produce at 35*s*. each hive, would give 1,792*l*. as their total value.

How many stocks may be kept in a given area, without overstocking, is a question often asked. We can only reply that we have never yet known any district overstocked. Wagner tells us the number of stocks kept on each square mile in the following countries: viz. Hanover, 141 stocks; province of Atica, in Greece, containing 45 square miles, 20,000 hives; a province in Holland, 2,000 stocks per square mile. No square mile in the British Islands can equal the above estimate, therefore we are justified in stating that we are not likely at our present slow rate of progress to over-populate any given area.

We should be glad if we could prevail upon our people to pay far more attention to bees. In both Italy and Spain they are extensively cultivated. We have read of a farmer in Spain who had 5,000 hives.

"A LIST OF PLANTS SUITABLE FOR BEE-CULTURE,

Excluding those commonly grown in the kitchen garden and orchard: compiled by Dr. Münter, director of the botanic garden of Greifswald." The following list, extracted from the above work, may be of interest to some of our readers who are bee-keepers. We may note that Greifswald lies in about 54° 5′ N. lat., and about 13° E. long., hence its spring is about a fortnight or three weeks later than in England:—

(Yielding honey, unless otherwise stated.)

I.—For the period from March 1 till the middle of April.

Erythronium Dens-canis
Scilla amœna
Galanthus nivalis
Leucojum vernum
Crocus vernus
Daphne Mezereum
Corylus tubulosa, pollen
Primula officinalis
Lamium maculatum (also pollen)
Pulmonaria officinalis
Symphytum orientale
Petasites niveus (also pollen)
   „ officinalis (also pollen)
Sambucus racemosus

Cornus mascula
Ribes Sanguineum
Viola odorata —
Saxifraga cæspitosa
   „ hypnoides
Arabis alpina (also pollen) -
Aubrietia columnæ (also pollen)
   „ deltoidea (also pollen)
   „ microstyla (also pollen)
Corydalis cava —
   „ solida
Eranthis hyemalis
Helleborus niger

II.—From the middle of April until the end of May.

Taxus baccata (pollen)
Picea alba (pollen)
Erythronium Dens-canis
Scilla amœna
Hyacinthus orientalis
Ornithogalum nutans
Fritillaria imperialis

Galanthus nivalis
Leucojum vernum
Crocus vernus
   „ germanica
   „ gramineus
Polygonum Bistorta (also pollen)
Daphne Mezereum

Primula officinalis
„ Auricula
Galeobdolon luteum
Lamium maculatum
Salvia pratensis
Symphytum orientale
Anchusa officinalis
Myosotis sylvatica
Petasites officinalis (also pollen)
„ niveus (also pollen)
Taraxacum officinale (also pollen)
Sambucus racemosus (pollen)
Fraxinus Ornus (also pollen)
Cornus mascula
Ribes sangineum
„ aureum
Saxifraga hypnoides
„ cæspitosa
„ crassifolia

Amygdalus nana
„ communis
Persica vulgaris
Prunus Armeniaca
„ Mahaleb
Orobus vernus
Æsculus hippocastanum
Geranium phæum (also wax)
Viola odorata
Arabis alpina
Aubrietia deltoidea
„ columnæ
„ microstyla
Barbarea vulgaris
Lunaria rediviva
„ biennis
Corydalis cava
„ solida
Helleborous fœtidus
Adonis vernalis (pollen)

III.—*From the beginning of June till the end of July.*

Allium Schœnoprasum
Fritillaria meleagris
Lilium Martagon
Asphodelus luteus
Polygonatum officinale
„ multiflorum
Iris graminea
„ germanica
„ pallida
„ sibirica
Polygonum Bistorta (also pollen)
Rheum undulatum (also pollen)
„ rhaponticum (also pollen)
Populus balsamifera propolis
Armeria maritima
Salvia pratensis
„ verticillata
Betonica officinalis
Melittis melissophyllum
Origanum creticum
„ Onites

Digitalis purpurea
„ ambigua
„ lutea
Veronica latifolia
Polemonium cœruleum
Syringa vulgaris
„ persica
Centaurea scabiosa
Valeriana officinalis
Diervilla canadensis
Lonicera Peryclymenum
„ caprifolium
Cratægus coccinea
„ nigra
Rosea lutea
„ spinosissima
Fragaria chilensis
„ grandiflora
„ virginiana
Cytisus Laburnum
Robinia Pseud-Acacia

PLANTS SUITABLE FOR BEE-CULTURE.

Pavia flava and carnea
Ruta graveolens
Dictamnus Fraxinella
Althæa officinalis
„ rosea
Reseda odorata
Sinapis alba and nigra

Isatis tinctoria
Papaver somniferum (pollen)
Berberis Aquifolium
Aquilegia vulgaris
Thalictrum flavum
T. aquilegifolium

IV.—*From the end of July till the middle of September.*

Anthericum ramosum (also pollen)
Gladiolus floribundus
Lilium candidum (also pollen)
Gladiolus gandavensis
Polygonum Sieboldii
Cannabis sativa (pollen)
Statice Limonium
Lavandula officinalis
Dracocephalum Moldavicum
Salvia æthiopis
„ hispanica
Monarda didyma
„ punctata
„ barbata
„ Kalmiana
Teucrium chamædrys
Leonurus cardiaca
Pentstemon barbatum
Nicotiana rustica
„ Tabacum
„ macrophylla
Physalis Alkekengi
Borago officinalis
Cerinthe major
„ gymnandra
Hydrophyllum virginicum
Phacelia congesta
Nolana paradoxa
Convolvulus tricolor
Ipomœa coccinea
Asclepias Syriaca
Campanula Medium
„ pyramidalis
„ carpatica

Lobelia Erinus
Solidago virg-aurea
Senecio sarracenicus
Helianthus annuus
„ argyrophyllus
Tagetes patula
Echinops exaltatus
„ sphærocephalus
Centaurea moschata
Sanvitalia procumbens
Ageratum mexicanum
Helenium pumilum
Silphium amplexicaule (pollen)
Cephalaria transsylvanica
Scabiosa lucida (pollen)
„ atropurpurea (pollen)
Sicyos angulata
Bryonia alba et dioica
Heuchera americana
„ divaricata
Sedum Fabaria
Portulaca oleracea propolis
Lythrum salicaria
„ flexuosum
Godetia albescens (pollen)
Clarkia pulchella
„ elegans
Œnothera Lamarckiana (also pollen
Epilobium angustifolium
Spirea hypericifolia
„ chamædrifolia
Rubus odoratus (pollen)
Rhus typhina (pollen)
Balsamina hortensis

Linum perenne	Bunias orientalis
Melianthus major	Macleya cordata (pollen)
Lavatera trimestris (pollen)	Delphinium Ajacis
,, thuringiaca (pollen)	,, grandiflorum
Kitaibelia vitifolia (also pollen)	Nigella sativa
Kölreuteria paniculata	,, damascena
Reseda odorata	,, hispanica
Hesperis matronalis	

Dr. Münter makes one more period—namely, from the middle of September till October, and includes the colchicums as well as some of the foregoing plants,—so much depends upon the weather after the beginning of September as to what bees will do.

POLLEN, OR BEE-BREAD.

Many erroneous notions prevail amongst bee-keepers respecting pollen. If you watch the entrance to the hive about noon on a very warm day in summer, you will perceive, if the hive is prosperous and possesses a fertile queen, many of the worker bees carrying in a quantity of yellow, brown, or reddish substance on their legs (in fact they are so heavily laden that they can scarcely fly)—this is often, though erroneously, supposed to be materials for making the wax. Walk round the garden border, and perhaps on one of the beds you will find some showy white lillies; upon examining the centre of the flower you will see a few yellowish-looking heads or knobs, supported on long stalks, these are what botanists call the stamens; the heads, which are filled with yellow powder, are known by the name of anthers; the stalks are the filaments, and the powder itself is pollen, or the fertilizing agent in plants. The anthers when ripe split up the sides, then the pollen grains fall upon the viscid or gluey stalk which you see exactly in the centre of the flower, called the stigma, so as to fertilise the young seeds; but in every flower there are many thousands of pollen grains more than are needed for the purpose of fertilisation; yet in nature nothing is wasted; the little industrious bee comes in for his share, often a lion's share. The bee uses the pollen not for making its combs to store the honey in, but only for feeding its young whilst in the larva or grub state. Some think it is eaten for food by the mature bees; this also is a mistake. Huber demonstrated very clearly that it was used only for the young brood. For example, he confined a colony of bees to the hive containing no honey, but having in the cells a great amount of pollen or bee-bread; the bees in a short time died, leaving the bee-bread untouched in the cells. Then he placed a large quantity of young hatched brood in the hive containing much honey but not a particle of pollen; the young brood all perished, and were found dead and decaying in the cells. This proves that the bee-bread gathered in a breeding season in such large quantities is used solely to nourish the brood.

Experiments have been made by Langstroth and others to test the disputed question as to whether the bees consume the bee-bread when building the comb, or only honey. It was found by Langstroth that bees confined in a hive with both honey and bee-bread, but without any brood in the cells, consumed both when rapidly secreting wax to build the combs; but Gundelach, a German bee-keeper, found that bees with a fertile queen, confined to the hive and supplied only with honey, rapidly built a comb, in which the queen deposited eggs; but, after the eggs were hatched, the young larva could not be fed with pollen—it died in every case within twenty-four hours.

Every intelligent bee-keeper will watch his hives most jealously early in the season, from the last week in January or the first week in February. If the bees are carrying no pollen to the hive the queen has not commenced to deposit her eggs. It is a joyous sign to the bee-master to see the little workers (really very small in size after the winter's idleness) loaded with pollen early in the year; he knows then that all is doing well inside the hive, the queen must be healthy, and it is also the best sign he can have that he may look for early swarms; but, if no bee-bread has been carried in by March, he should begin to suspect that something is wrong. The hive ought to be at once overhauled, the queen examined —most probably the hive under these circumstances will be found queenless.

If the worker bee is carefully observed, it will be seen covered with small hairs, and if followed to the flower where pollen is abundant it will be seen to roll itself over the anthers, or by going down the tubes of the flower the pollen dust falls upon it, then it scrapes as it were the pollen off its legs, and gathers it together in a hollow (in bee-books called a basket) on the thigh. When the laden bee has returned to the hive, it somehow attracts the attention of others; these, perhaps engaged in feeding the larva, take a portion, sometimes all the pollen, from its legs. This may be required for immediate use, as suggested by Langstroth; however, the hard-worked bee is not always aided in unloading, for often when the pollen is being brought to the hive in abundance the bee has to take and press it down one of the cells. It is very interesting to watch this operation; it places the lower half of the body in the cell and scrapes off the pollen with its legs in the same manner that it pressed it on the thighs when in the flower. Not unfrequently the bee finds it difficult to press the pollen in lumps on its legs; then in this dilemma it rolls amongst the anthers, and returns to the hive with its body thickly covered with the powder. We have tried to find out the reason for this non-adhesiveness of the pollen dust; at first we thought it must be because of moisture, as it will be observed that large quantities of the powder are thus carried early in the morning succeeding a rainy day; but I have since discovered that many plants produce pollen which is not adhesive under any circumstances; such pollen, when examined with high power under the microscope, is found to be spherical (like an orange). Other grains, such as the crocus, snowdrop, &c., which are oblong in shape are very adhesive, but that from the dandelion and many composite flowers is non-adhesive. The pollen from the mallow, the cheese-cakes of children, is very beautiful when magnified; studded over with a multitude of sharp points, resembling thorns, thus making it very adhesive.

When more bee-bread is collected than is sufficient for the immediate use of the brood, it is stored away in worker cells; first it is tightly pressed down in the cell by the head of the bee, until the cell is rather more than two-thirds full. Over the bee-bread a little honey is placed, afterwards the cell is sealed up with wax, to await a rainy day, or a time when the pollen is scarce. An immense number of the cells are found in old hives in winter, when the whole colony is resting from their labours, partly filled with bee-bread. These are unsealed, and the cells are never sealed or covered over with wax unless filled either with young brood, honey, or bee-bread.

If something could be discovered that would supply the place of the bee-bread in early spring, so as to induce the queen to deposit her eggs shortly after Christmas or at the beginning of the new year, it would be hailed with delight by every intelligent bee-keeper. It is true the German apiarians supply their stocks in February with finely-ground rye-flour, and it is said the bees carry it into their hives with evident pleasure. Dzierzon first made the discovery by observing his colonies carry it into the hives from a mill close by. If the queen can be persuaded to deposit her eggs early in the season, it must have the effect of strengthening the stocks with young bees, and they become exceedingly strong just when the honey-harvest is commencing; thus a great advantage is gained. Many stocks are, comparatively speaking, worthless, simply because weak through being late hatched. It should be borne in mind, when seeking a substitute for pollen, that it is a substance highly nitrogenous; both unbolted wheaten, rye, and barley flour contain a fair proportion of nitrogen, and might be serviceable in very late seasons. A good plan to feed the hives with flour is to place it on a large dinner-plate at a little distance from the apiary, and on stands about the same height from the ground as the hives, care being especially exercised to keep the flour very dry and free from moisture.

Each bee collects apparently only from one kind of plant. We judge this, because if they gathered it from several different kinds of plants the pollen would doubtless be of several colours. After most careful scrutiny I have never observed a bee with more than one colour of pollen on its legs.

The bees in spring, when new pollen begins to be plentiful, although they may have a large stock of last year's pollen in the hive, disregard this and prefer the new bee-bread; but, if unfavourable weather comes on, the old pollen rapidly disappears.

Our large timber or forest trees yield a rich harvest of bee-bread for the bees. About one of the first trees which afford aid to the hives is the elm; long before its leaves appear the naked branches are clothed with thousands of clusters of reddish-looking flowers, and one of the most pleasant sounds in early spring is the hum of bees gathering pollen from the elm avenue, especially on a fine day, warmed with the sun's genial rays. Amongst the crocus, anemone, and snowdrop beds the bees collect their first and earliest supply of pollen; and, as soon as these are fading, the lesser celandine puts in an appearance on every sunny bank. This was Wordsworth's favourite flower:—

> "The first gilt thing
> That wears the trembling pearls of spring."

Wordsworth, Nature's poet, hailed this humble blossom every spring with great delight. By some disease of the respiratory organs he was confined the greater part of the winter to his house, but, when the warm days of spring came again, he felt pleased to be in the fields, where generally the first plant he hailed and welcomed too as a harbinger of bright and warmer days was the lesser celandine. Then the dandelion and daisy follow in rapid succession, and the fields are shortly clad with a golden dress of buttercups:—

> "Buttercups and daisies,
> Oh, the pretty flowers,
> Coming in the spring time
> To tell of sunny hours.
> When the trees are leafless,
> When the fields are bare,
> Glossy golden buttercups
> Spring up here and there."

No sooner does the month of May (the flowery month of our forefathers) come in than the pollen-gatherers find plenty to do—from this month until September there is no scarcity of bee-bread. The honey-harvest may and often does fail by the beginning of August, but the flowers must yield pollen long afterwards. The latest that I can ever remember the bees to be collecting bee-bread was until November in 1869.

It is but seldom the florist, horticulturist, or farmer thinks how greatly he is indebted to the little honey and pollen-gatherer for his beautiful flowers, rich luscious fruits, and splendid seed-harvests. Many flowers cannot be fertilised; no perfect seeds or fruits can be produced without the direct agency of insects. It has been proved without doubt that many stone fruits cannot "set" without the bee conveying pollen to the stigma. In springs when much unfavourable cold weather prevails, accompanied with easterly winds, the honey-bee very seldom under such circumstances leaves the hive; in the meantime, the plum, damson, and cherry trees have bloomed without the usual friendly visits of the bee, the consequence being great scarcity of these fruits. The farmer will probably say: "Oh, it is the fault of the cold easterly winds;" it may be so, we freely confess, so far as confining and making involuntary prisoners of the poor bees; for, if the bees had been able to sing their cheerful hum amid the flowers, there would have been no scarcity of fruits. The bee is often much blamed in the south of Europe for eating the tender grapes; the bee is not able, however, to bite the outer skin, but it does eat the soft pulp inside the tough skin when it finds any fruits that are bruised. The wasp or hornet are the real enemies to fruits, and not the bee; they are provided with strong jaws for sawing wood, of which their cells are composed, where the larva is reared in their nests; but the honey-bee has not the strong saw-like jaws of the wasp, and is wholly incapable of injuring the most tender fruits. Watch the wasp, or rather the hornet, on the pear-trees, eating the finest and most ripe fruit it can find, and you will at once discover the real "rascal," and the worst thief the horticulturist has to deal with.

PROPOLIS, OR HIVE CEMENT AND VARNISH.

The fact that bees are excellent architects and builders has been known from very early times. The greater part of their building is composed of wax, but as houses require besides bricks and stones cement or mortar, so bees also have their cement, which they use to fasten securely the new and delicate combs to the top of the hive; not only so, they make their dwelling both wind and water tight, by cementing up most securely even the smallest crevice or opening, though not larger than a pin's head. As our polishers and painters to complete their work varnish it over, so the bees, when the cells are complete—if not immediately tenanted and filled either with honey, beebread, or the young bees—coat them over with a thin film of varnish. About the end of March or commencement of April, a little before sundown, the atmosphere is sometimes filled with a balsamic perfume, a pleasant hum is distinctly audible, unheard in the busy part of the day; the perfume arises from the balsam poplar, whose leaf-buds are now, under the genial influence of spring, rapidly expanding; the gum or gluey substance, which coated the buds like hard varnish, and rendered them impervious to wintry rains, frost, and snow, is being eagerly gathered by the bees; hence the humming sound.

Why do they collect this sticky stuff? was a question once placed before the writer. The answer cannot be better given than by quoting the experience of the learned though blind Huber. One spring, to observe their mode of gathering the gum, he planted in pots near his apiary a quantity of the branches of the balsam poplar, before the buds were expanded. "The bees alighted on them, separated the folds of the large buds with their forceps, extended the varnish in threads, and loaded first one thigh and then the other, for they convey it like pollen, transferring it from the first pair of legs to the second, by which it is lodged in the hollow of the third."

This cement, gathered like pollen from many sources, is called "propolis;" it is a very hard substance, at least it hardens soon after it is employed by the bees. I have seen perforated zinc used at the top of the hive for feeding, &c. when uncovered for a few days become coated over with propolis, so hard and tough that it is necessary to employ a sharp knife to detach it from the zinc plate. It is principally the gummy exudation of trees, from leaf-buds and bark; sometimes when doors are newly varnished bees will eagerly scrape off the varnish to use as propolis, and they have been known to gather the pitch from boats and vessels as they are floating up canals. A friend of mine who keeps an apiary on the banks of a canal was at first puzzled to account for his bees working about the masts and ropes of the barges that were going to and fro, and returning laden with a brownish substance on their legs, which he thought for a long time was pollen; in this case it was a mixture in which pitch mingled largely. In the summer of 1868 I was preparing a jar of Venice turpentine. After melting the resin and mingling with it the turpentine, I unthinkingly left it exposed in my garden walk. Whilst very hot it emits a strong odour, which may be detected at a long distance; this attracted my poor bees, who, no doubt, thinking they were about to gather rich spoils of propolis, alighted on the surface and were as quickly killed. The slaughter was very great; I found not less than 1500 bees destroyed. The jar was filled to the brim with dead and dying bees.

The hollyhock buds yield a supply of propolis, which

the bees largely appropriate; they collect it also from the birch and alder bark, and in abundance from the bark of various firs and pines. In spring the horse-chestnut buds are large and conspicuous; when unfolding the gummy matter is softened, and this the industrious insects pick off. This gum has been known to entrap small birds, notably the golden-crested wren, in the same manner as birdlime, yet it can be carried away by the small weak bee. Such is the fact, for I never yet saw a bee fastened to it, although I have searched on the buds expecting this result.

It takes a much longer time for them to collect this worthless product than either honey or pollen, therefore if a substitute to save this waste of time can be placed within easy access, or close to the apiary, by all means let it be done. Langstroth says, "To men time is money, to bees it is honey;" not only is time lost in collecting it, but it takes a much greater time to make use of it, from its glutinous or tough character. A composition of one part of bees-wax with three of resin has been recommended to be placed in a dish beside the apiary. We have, however, thought that if this composition was made and placed near the hives, like everything else collected by bees, they would not rest contented until it was all carried off, and inside the hives would soon be one mass of propolis; in the end it would become a perfect nuisance, both to the bees and all cleanly apiarians. For my part, speaking, too, from experience, what they require let them gather, but do not leave any newly-varnished work unwatched or unguarded until perfectly hard, when it will defy all attacks.

The most important use to which propolis is applied by bees is to fasten securely the newly-made combs. They use it also for other purposes. About August, 1869, I witnessed in a neighbouring apiary a deadly struggle going on betwixt a colony of bees in a common straw hive and wasps. The entrance or mouth of the hive was, as is too often the case in cottagers' skeps, too large, no attempt being made by the owner to make it less, so as to give the bees a better chance to defend their home against the wily enemies, who were rapidly depopulating the hive and eating up their hoarded winter's store of honey. I anxiously watched the result from day to day, and in the end I was much pleased by seeing the bees victorious. I placed a small pebble in the mouth of the hive to contract the entrance a little, and the following fact will show the foresight of these marvellous insects. They went out in crowds to a fir plantation, so I supposed, about half a mile distant, and returned laden with propolis; by degrees, but quickly, considering the circumstances, the mouth was built up and narrowed, so that only about three bees could pass and repass at one time. Then the bees were quite prepared to fight for their queen and colony. Two or three sentinels were placed on the alighting board, who appeared to give warning to those inside when an enemy was in sight, and if he attempted to enter he was compelled to beat a hasty retreat. This hive became a valuable stock the following season, and was sold by the fortunate owner for a goodly sum.

Other uses are found for this cement. Maraldi, on one occasion, found a large black snail had worked its way into the interior of one of his wooden hives. The bees stung it so fiercely as to cause its death. The next question was how to remove its large slimy body, which if left inside the heated hive would soon putrefy and become offensive; in this extremity, they, as if by agreement, neglected the other work of the hive, and went forth in a strong body. Maraldi for a time was left in doubt as to their intention; however, they soon returned laden with propolis, which they applied to the dead body, and thus coated it over with an impervious cement, rendering it inoffensive.

Another snail story is recorded by Dr. Bevan as having occurred in the apiary of M. Réaumur. A garden-snail with hard shell crawled one evening through the entrance of the hive, apparently unnoticed by the sentinels guarding the entrance; at least, having a hard shell, the bees, we should judge, were unable to destroy it by their stings. Next morning M. Réaumur observed it resting with slime upon the glass with which one side of the hive was covered; at the same moment he noticed the bees were wild and excited, evidently disliking their strange visitor, who had so coolly taken up his quarters as a tenant in their home, and as the sequel will show he was destined to be a permanent fixture in the hive, for they applied propolis dexterously around the edge of the shell in contact with the glass; this when hardened was as firm as cement, and securely fastened the snail to the glass, so that he was unable to stir from the spot where he had ensconced himself.

I have heard of the body of a mouse being encased in propolis similar to the snail, but cannot vouch for it as a fact.

Bees collect propolis in the greatest quantity about noon. It is very seldom gathered either in the early morning or in the evening, whilst honey and pollen are both brought to the hive at all hours. Propolis can be collected best in the heat of the day, when softened by the sun. According to Vanquelin, who analysed it direct from the hive, it consists of one part of wax to four of resin. When brought to the hive it is of a soft, pliant nature, but in a few hours so rapidly does it harden that ofttimes it is difficult for the bees to tear it away from the legs of those who have gathered it. When an old-fashioned cottager's skep has stood on the stand for a few months it is so firmly glued down with propolis as to be immovable, except a knife is passed between the straw and the stand; even if it be loosened they are not long in again securing it, perhaps led by some instinctive dread lest their home with its beloved contents should be swept off by a gale of wind.

I stated above, propolis is gathered from many sources. Mr. Knight observed his bees tearing away the varnish, composed of wax and turpentine, which he had applied over the trunks of some of his trees where the bark had been lost, and Dr. Evans spent many hours watching them gather the viscid substance found on hollyhock buds. He states they would rest ten minutes on the same bud, first moulding the substance with the fore-feet, then transferring it to the hind legs, somewhat after the same manner that pollen is gathered.

Propolis is never stored in the cells for future use; it is gathered when most needed by the colony. For example, Réaumur placed a new swarm in a hive made of wood and glass. The glass was carelessly fastened only with paper and paste. The bees immediately discovered this defect, and saw the glass was insecure, therefore they indignantly gnawed away the paper and fastened the glass securely with propolis.

Insects of all kinds seem to abhor turpentine, and look upon it in the same light that we should regard poison; but bees frequently gather it when mingled with either wax or resin, as in the varnish used by Mr. Knight to his trees.

HOW TO AVOID THE BRIMSTONE-PIT.

No apiarian has laboured more effectually for the abolition of the brimstone-pit among cottagers than the late Rev. W. C. Cotton. About the year 1838 he sent out two letters addressed especially to the cottage bee-keepers of England, containing much practical good sense and advice, under the title of a "Bee-Preserver." He afterwards collected other information and valuable notes upon apiculture, which, together with the two before-named letters, he incorporated into a volume called "My Bee Book."

Mr. Cotton's plan was to stupefy the bees with the fumes produced by burning puff balls, or puff fungus, a plant not uncommonly seen in fields in the autumn, gathered half-ripe and carefully dried; then to shake out the bees, cut out the combs, and replace the bees in the hive, and in the evening, having fumigated another full hive, to introduce into it the bees out of the combless hive.

This method, though it has doubtless proved serviceable to many cottagers, is not so easy as the simple driving system, which I will now describe.

HOW TO DRIVE BEES.

Choose a fine warm day between 10 A.M. and 1 P.M., when the bees are actively engaged working in the fields. First prepare two empty straw hives, one of them as nearly resembling in shape and size the stock to be operated upon as possible—a long roller towel with the seam removed so as to be used in one length—a long piece of strong cord, a small roll of linen rags, and a bucket. Inexperienced persons are recommended to wear a bee dress. Stand the bucket firmly on the ground, two or three yards from the condemned hive, and having lighted the roll of linen rags with a match, so as to cause it to smoulder and produce a good quantity of smoke, then gently blow the smoke into the entrance of the hive; just a few whiffs are sufficient. Having done this, frequently the cottage hive, especially if it has stood on the bench unmolested for a couple of years, will be found to be firmly fastened with propolis to the stand; if so, pass a knife betwixt the board and the hive all round. Then lift up the hive and blow a few puffs of smoke amongst the combs to cause the bees to retire to the top of the hive. At this stage of the process the bees will not be inclined to fly about; on the contrary they are generally very peaceable. Now carefully carry the hive and place it in the bucket, with the crown downwards, at the same instant covering it with one of the empty hives, and wind around the part where the two hives join, the roller towel, to prevent any bees from escaping, and tie it firmly on with a cord (four turns of the string is sufficient, two around the lower and two around the upper hive). Having proceeded thus far successfully, you may rest a moment, not forgetting at this stage to place on the stand exactly where the hive stood the other empty hive; this will perhaps prevent fighting with the other stocks, and cause the bees who have been out working to enter it.

If the day be sultry, and working hard in the sun unpleasant, remove the bucket containing the two hives to some shady spot, beneath a tree if possible, and commence drumming smartly with both hands on the lower hive, at the bottom of which the bees are gathered; for directly bees are surrounded with or smell the smoke they become terrified and rush to the top of their hive, where the honey cells are generally found, to fill their honey bags. The bees, if a constant drumming is kept up, are not long in quitting their domicile, and clustering on the top of the empty hive; generally speaking the driving is complete in fifteen minutes, although sometimes it is very difficult to make them quit their old hive. It must never be attempted on a dull rainy day; choose only a fine and warm day, smoke well, and the driving is easy. After beating the under hive for a quarter of an hour, unloose the towel, and look carefully inside the hives if all the bees are seen clustering like a swarm on the top of the empty skep, except perhaps a few stragglers; remove the hive now containing the bees to the stand, to take the place of the old skep, and leave it there until evening. When driving put your ear close to the top hive, and listen; if the swarming hum (a peculiarly sweet sound made by the wings) is heard, all is going on satisfactorily. But, if no humming sound is audible, they have not been terrified or smoked sufficiently. The few bees left amongst the combs may be either shaken out on the ground, or, what is better still, brushed out with a feather; they will not be long in returning to their companions on the stand.

Now attend to the hive with the combs. If it is left in the neighbourhood of the bee-house an hour or two, probably very little honey will be found in it when wanted. Remove it at once to a cool room where the bees have no access. It is also a wise plan to drain out the honey from the combs after nightfall, to prevent robbing by the bees; it is very unpleasant to have them buzzing around the room, which they most certainly will be if honey is scented in working hours.

UNITING STOCKS.

The driven bees will not do much good if left to themselves, without comb and honey, and with winter coming on. Examine all the remaining stocks; very likely you have a second swarm (often called a cast), which are weak and contain but few bees. You will do well to strengthen these, or any weak stock you have in the apiary, by uniting with them the driven bees. In the evening again put a match to the linen rags, and blow a few whiffs of smoke into the weak hive in which you purpose placing the condemned stock. Spread on the ground opposite the hive a tablecloth, on which place two walking-sticks, or other supports, for the hive to rest upon, so that no bees will be crushed, and with a sudden blow knock out all the bees in the combless hive betwixt the two sticks, and as quickly as possible lift the weak hive from the stand and put it on the sticks over the bees. The bees scrambling over the cloth will not be long in seeking shelter in the hive, where they generally receive a hearty welcome. Next morning, when you remove it to the stand, one of the queens will be found dead on the cloth; the strongest as a rule will be the reigning queen in the double hive. The bees when mixed together or united are very seldom known to fight. I have not known a single instance of fighting, although I have in the autumn for several years united a great number. I have had seven distinct stocks thus mingled, so as to form one large colony.

If there is the slightest chance that the bees will not be received kindly when united as above, adopt another plan. Soon after you have driven the first stock, smoke the weak stock, and drive them in the same way you proceeded with the condemned stock, only drive them into the same hive, so that they both are alike terrified and alarmed, and mingle peaceably together. Then, at once, do not wait for evening, knock them out upon the cloth, and place the original hive, with combs, &c., over them, and they will ascend, joyfully humming their delightful song of peace. Thus, with very little trouble, you will secure a good stock of bees. If they winter well, and come out healthy in the spring, they will probably send out an early and strong swarm, besides being in good condition for securing the honey harvest, whereas the weak colony would have done very little good; nay, I have invariably found them to cost more in watching and feeding than they were worth.

PART II.

INHABITANTS OF THE HIVE.

NOTES AND HINTS ABOUT BEES.

To persons not much acquainted with bees the following notes and hints may be useful:—

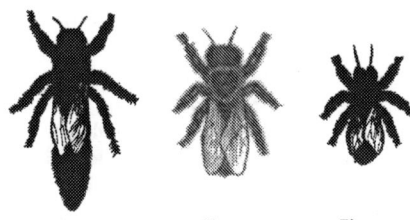

Fig. 1.   Fig. 2.   Fig. 3.

Fig. 1. The *Queen Bee:* the head is of a triangular shape; her wings very short, not extending beyond the one-half of her body, which is longer, and more pointed, than that of the working bees. Her legs and corselet are copper-coloured; thorax grey, and abdomen brown. There is only one queen to a hive; while there are from 10,000 to 15,000 workers, and perhaps 1000 or 1200 drones.

Fig. 2. The *Drone*, or Male Bee; the head is round, its large body is almost entirely covered by its wings. It has no sting. The drones appear only at the season of swarming, and are all put to death by the workers in the autumn.

Fig. 3. The *Working Bee*. Head somewhat triangular; the smallest and most numerous of the hive, which every one knows as the *honey-bee*. It builds the combs, makes the honey, and feeds the young.

Queen-bees are matured on the fourteenth day from the egg being deposited in the royal cells, and will usually begin to lay eggs fourteen days after maturity.

Worker Bees are matured in twenty-one days from the egg.

Drones require twenty-four days from the egg.

Stock Hives are without brood on the twenty-fourth day after swarming, which is the best time to turn them out, if this be desirable.

Casts, or *Second Swarms*, need not be watched for later than the tenth or fourteenth day after a natural swarm. Second swarms are always preceded by piping.

Third Swarms will occasionally follow the second, either the same or the following day: but should always be returned the same evening to the old hive.

Situation of Apiary must always be in a sheltered spot; *be sure about this*.

Keep your Stocks strong: without this it is impossible to succeed as a Bee-farmer.

A moderate increase of stocks every year is the best plan.

Always smoke the hive before meddling with the combs.

Bees gorged with honey never venture to attack any one; they are, therefore, quite harmless and quiet when swarming.

Weigh every Hive in September, and feed up to about 18 lbs.

Ventilate your hives thoroughly at commencement of the winter.

Cleanliness is most important. Be sure to keep hives, extractor, feeder, &c. clean.

Watch your hives as keenly as the bees do against enemies, such as moth, wasps, mice, &c. in *September* and *October*.

Make entrance very small in winter, and enlarge it as required in summer.

Transfer a new swarm both to the hive and stand they are to occupy permanently on the day they issue from the old hive.

Distance between your hives should be about three feet.

Fighting. If you perceive any hive being robbed, close the entrance for twenty-four hours; if the fighting continues, remove the hive some distance away.

Luck. No such thing is known in bee-management, it is care and forethought.

Try again. If you are disgusted with the old system and have given it up in despair, let us persuade you to *try again;* you may depend upon having a generous return for your trouble if you follow the calling of a bee-farmer faithfully.

THE QUEEN-BEE.

The queen-bee, very appropriately called in Germany the mother-bee, is the only perfectly developed female bee in the hive. She is easily known from the other bees by the greater length of her body, her peculiar short wings, and the longer legs are not provided with baskets like the worker bee. The abdomen tapers to a point, and her sting is curved, but she is recognised by her slow majestic walk, and, when she moves about the comb, her subjects form in a circle round her.

A queen in the height of the working season is estimated to lay from 1,500 to 2,000 eggs each day, and every year is supposed to produce at least 100,000 bees. This enormous number is probably not an over-estimate.

It is remarkable that the homage or deference paid to the queen is not lavished on an unwedded or unfertile queen, for the inmates of the hive appear to know the difference. Dr. Dunbar strikingly illustrates this: "So long as the queen remained a virgin, not the slightest degree of respect or attention was paid to her; not a single bee gave her food; she was obliged, as often as she required it, to help herself, and in crossing the honey-cells for that purpose she had to scramble, often with difficulty, over the crowd, not an individual of which got out of her way, or seemed to care whether she fed or starved; but no sooner did she become a mother than the scene was changed, and all testified towards her that most affectionate attention which is uniformly exhibited to fertile queens."

> "But mark her royal port and awful mien,
> Where moves with measured pace the insect queen.
> Twelve chosen guards, with slow and solemn gait,
> Bend at her nod, and round her person wait."
> —*Evans.*

Though provided with a sting like the worker-bee, she never uses it in self-defence, excepting only in combat with a rival queen. Not unfrequently, after the first swarm has left the hive, which is always led by the old queen, she leaves behind her two or three young queens in the cells; and it may occur that two of them leave the cell at the same time; in that case, if the hive is not sufficiently populous to throw off another swarm, the two queens fight; the victor reigns afterwards supreme over the colony. In this case, Huber states, she uses her sting to destroy her rival.

The queen lays the eggs, which may produce workers, drones, or queens. Langstroth, the noted American apiarian, who has devoted many years to the study of bees, says, "It has been noticed that the queen-bee usually commences laying very early in the season, and always long before there are any males in the hive." How, then, are her eggs impregnated? Francis Huber, of Geneva, by a long course of indefatigable investigations,

THE QUEEN-BEE.

threw much light upon this subject. He ascertained that, like many other insects, she was fecundated in the open air and on the wing, and that the effect lasts for several years, and probably for life. To his amazement he found that unwedded queens laid eggs, but they always produced drones. He tried this experiment repeatedly, but always with the same result. Bee-keepers, even from the time of Aristotle, had observed that all the brood in a hive were occasionally drones. Before attempting to explain this astonishing fact, I must call the attention of the reader to another of the mysteries of the bee-hive.

It has always been stated that the workers are proved by dissection to be females, which, under ordinary circumstances, are barren. Occasionally some of them appear to be sufficiently developed to be capable of laying eggs; but these eggs, like those of unwedded queens, always produce drones. Sometimes, when a colony which has lost its queen despairs of obtaining another, these drone-laying workers are exalted to her place, and treated with equal regard by the bees.

The eggs of bees are of a lengthened, oval shape, with a slight curvature, and of a bluish white colour. Being besmeared at the time of laying with a glutinous substance, they adhere to the bases of the cells, and remain unchanged in figure, or situation, for three or four days; they are then hatched, the bottom of each cell presenting to view a small white worm. On its growing, so as to touch the opposite angle of each cell, it coils itself up, to use the language of Swammerdam, like a dog when going to sleep, and floats in a whitish transparent fluid, which is deposited in the cells by the nursing bees, and by which it is probably nourished; it becomes gradually enlarged in its dimensions till the two extremities touch one another and form a ring. In this state it is called a larva or worm. So nicely do the bees calculate the quantity of food which will be required that none remains in the cell when it is transformed into a nymph. It is the opinion of many eminent naturalists that pollen does not constitute the sole food of the grub, but that it consists of a mixture of pollen, honey, and water, partly digested in the stomachs of the nursing bees: one point is clear, it is highly nitrogenous.

The larva, having derived its support in the manner above described for four, five, or six days, according to the season, continues to increase during that period till it occupies the whole breadth or length of the cell. The nursing bees now seal over the cell with a light brown cover, externally more or less convex (the cap of a drone-cell being more convex than that of a worker-cell), and thus differing from that of a honey cell, which is paler and somewhat concave. The larva is no sooner perfectly inclosed than it begins to line the cell, by spinning round itself, after the manner of a silkworm, a whitish silky film or cocoon, by which it is encased as it were in a pod. When it has undergone this change it is generally called nymph or larva. It has now attained its full growth, and the large amount of nutriment which it has taken serves as a store for developing the perfect insect.

The working-bee nymph spins its cocoon in thirty-six hours. After passing about three days in this state of preparation for a new existence it gradually undergoes so great a change as not to bear a vestige of its previous form.

When it has reached the twenty-first day of its existence, counting from the time the egg was laid, it comes forth a perfect winged insect. The cocoon is left behind and forms a closely attached and exact lining to the cell in which it was spun. By this means the breeding-cells become smaller, and their partitions stronger, the oftener they change their tenants, and may become so much diminished in size as not to admit of the perfect development of full-sized bees. Such are the respective stages of

THE QUEEN-BEE.

the working-bee. Those of the *royal cell* are as follows: she passes three days in the egg, and is five a worm; the workers then close her cell, and she immediately begins spinning her cocoon, which occupies her twenty-four hours; in the tenth and eleventh days and part of the twelfth, as if exhausted by her labour, she remains in complete repose. Then she passes four days and part of the fifth as a nymph. It is on the sixteenth day, therefore, that the perfect state of queen is attained.

The drone passes three days in the egg, and six and a-half as a worm, and changes into a perfect insect on the twenty-fourth or twenty-fifth day after the egg is laid.

The development of each insect proceeds more slowly when the colonies are weak or the air cool. Dr. Hunter has observed that the eggs, worms, or nymphs all require a heat above $70°$ Fah. for their evolution. Both drones and workers, on emerging from the cell, are at first grey, soft, and comparatively helpless, so that some time elapses before they take wing. The workers and drones spin complete cocoons, or inclose themselves on every side, while the royal larvæ construct only imperfect cocoons, open behind, and enveloping only the head, thorax, and first ring of the abdomen, and Huber concludes, without hesitation, that the final cause of this is, that they may be exposed to the mortal sting of the first hatched queen, whose instinct leads her instantly to seek the destruction of those who would soon become her rivals.

If the royal larvæ spun complete cocoons, the sting of the queen seeking to destroy her rivals might be so entangled in their meshes that it could not be disengaged. "Such," says Huber, "is the instinctive enmity of young queens to each other, that I have seen one of them, immediately on its emergence from the cell, rush to those of its sisters, and tear to pieces even the imperfect larvæ. Hitherto philosophers have claimed our admiration of

Nature for her care in preserving and multiplying the species. But from these facts we must now admire her precautions in exposing certain individuals to a mortal hazard."[*]

The queen bee may survive five or six years, but she is not so productive after the third year. In ordinary years, in our climate, she ceases laying in October, and commences again in January, or, as is sometimes the case in very cold springs, in February. It is curious to note that when enfeebled with age she still lays abundantly, but the eggs produce only *drones*.

Hives such as the bar-frame hives, which allow the queen to be removed when the bees can raise another and younger queen from the worker brood, are invaluable to practical *bee-farmers*.

THE WORKER-BEE.

The worker-bee is an imperfectly-developed queen or female. They vary in number, for in a prosperous colony they may number above fifteen thousand, whilst in a weak hive there may be no more than ten thousand. Some writers have divided them into several sections, according to their work or tasks assigned them in the hive; thus they have nurses, wax-makers, ventilators, honey-collectors, &c. This we believe to be only imaginary, for every bee in the course of its life may undertake each of the above divisions of labour.

This, the hard-working member of the industrious hive, is very short-lived. Dr. Bevan thinks the limit of its age to be from six to eight months. When we consider the immense numbers killed by accident or eaten by birds we are astonished to think how the strength

[*] Bevan.

of the hive can be kept up, without taking into account the large numbers required to make up the two or three swarms annually sent out to commence house-keeping on their own account.

However, nothing seems to us so pitiable as an aged worker-bee with its torn wings striving some warm day in early spring to again attempt the collection of pollen or honey; rising feebly from the entrance, it sinks to the ground to die a miserable death—a sad end after its fruitful toils.

The worker is the stinging bee; by the sting it defends the hive to the death, and it never survives the use of this weapon of defence.

We need say but little about its well-known industry. Pettigrew thus touchingly notices this grand trait in their character: "Imagine a large and prosperous hive full of comb, bees, and brood; fancy 20,000 little grubs in this hive requiring constant attention and proper food, and all receiving them in due season; fancy the care and diligence of the bees in mixing and kneading this food before they give it to their young; fancy 2,000 of these grubs daily requiring and receiving beautiful lids on their cells, to cover them up whilst they pass into the insect form and chrysalis state; fancy 800 or 1,000 square inches of this brood being built up every three weeks; stand and look at that beehive, and remember that all therein goes on with unerring exactness and without light; then think of the untiring energy and perseverance of the bees outside the hive, ranging fields and woods from morn till dewy eve, gathering up the sweets and pollen of flowers, storing the one in sacks the other in baskets, returning to their home laden as donkeys with panniers, increasing their honey-store in weight from two to six pounds per day, securely locked up after it has been twice swallowed and disgorged, and thus made into honey proper." What a world of wonders is in a beehive!! The more we think over its wonders the more do we love these hard-working members of the ever-busy hive.

If apiarians had given a moment's thought to the fact that an ordinary worker-bee cannot survive over nine months, they would never have constructed the enormous hives which are now being sold so very extensively; especially when we consider that only one queen exists in the hive, from which all the workers must spring.

DRONES.

These insects, the non-working or non-producing part of the colony, are often regarded by the apiarian as a nuisance. Many good and apparently flourishing stocks have been destroyed or brought to a state of poverty and destitution by these idlers.

We are sometimes led to question the utility of so many in the hive, when we consider that only one is required to fertilize the virgin queen, and yet in many hives that we have kept there have been thousands; these, instead of diminishing as the season advanced, have often, until August, gone on increasing rapidly week by week. The earlier the drones begin to appear, the earlier we may, as a rule, expect swarms. The great laying of drone-eggs by a vigorous young queen generally takes place in the early part of April.

The drones, as most people are aware, are male bees. Fortunately they possess no stings, and may be handled with impunity. Their age is much less than that of the workers; they are also much larger than the workers, but they seem to be clumsy, and when on the wing make a loud buzzing noise. If the stocks are closely watched on a fine summer afternoon, they may be observed leaving the mouth of the hive by hundreds; this is for the purpose of meeting with the queens, who also leave the hive at about the same hour.

WHY SO MANY DRONES ARE PRODUCED.

If each stock of bees produced only one drone during the season, the chances are very much against the queen being able to meet *this one* in the air when she sallies out to meet her mate; and, if her Majesty was thus compelled to go out day by day in succession for a lengthened period, very likely she would be gobbled up by some hungry bird in search of a meal, or be destroyed in some other way—to say the least, her life would be jeopardised. But thousands of drones are hatched in most hives, so that the queen is seldom compelled to make more than one flight; for at the time she flies abroad there are scores if not hundreds of males buzzing here and there in the vicinity of the apiary. Thus impregnation takes place in the majority of instances on her first flight from the hive.

STRANGE THEORIES RESPECTING DRONES.

Many strange theories have been given to the world by professional apiarians which have no foundation in fact, such as the following: It has been asserted they are produced to fertilise the eggs as fast as the queen deposits them in the cells; others state they are nurses, or prepare the food for and feed the larvæ; others declare they sit upon the eggs and hatch them like birds; whereas others, and these latter have been a very numerous class, believe they are produced for the purpose of keeping up the temperature in the hive. It seems never to have struck the minds of these writers that the queen lays her eggs long before any drones make their appearance in the apiary in the early part of the year. Who or what fertilised these?

Again, how were the larvæ nursed or fed in early spring, and again late in autumn after the destruction of the drones? This needs no answer, and Dr. Evans is certainly mistaken in his theory. The same with the other theories, for they are merely theories, which every sensible bee-keeper now knows to be foolish.

We know no work on apiculture more readable than that written by Huish, but we are sorry to state he is far from trustworthy as a guide in many particulars: for example, what will our intelligent bee-keeping readers say to the following extract: "If by any accident or untoward event a hive be deficient in drones, the fecundation of the eggs of the queen does not take place, and consequently no swarms are produced?" All our readers know perfectly well, at least that portion of them who have taken delight in apiarian pursuits, that hundreds, if not thousands, of the busy industrious little workers are hatched and reared long before the drones make their appearance every season.

Huish also states: "When a hive swarms a number of drones follow the emigrants, in proportion to the number of working bees." We are quite prepared to admit that some few drones are generally found in the swarm, but this is the result of accident; they are not needful to the swarm. And swarms will be produced whether drones exist in the hive or not. We have had one instance ourselves, when we carefully extracted all the drone-cells as fast as they were made; not a drone was reared during the whole summer, yet it sent out a very heavy swarm the first week in June.

We not long ago read a continental work on bees, and were much amused with the curious statements made by the writer, statements that could only have been the creation of a fertile brain. For instance, when speaking upon this subject, he very gravely asserts that drones are constantly engaged carrying water for the colony, or words to this effect. We wonder whether he had watched them engaged in this aqueous exercise, and what kind of vessels they used when employed as water-carriers.

APPEARANCE OF DRONE-BEES.

Dr. Bevan, as well as other English authors, tell us that drones make their appearance in April. But the time varies very much, according to the season or the strength of the stocks. We have several years seen them in April; in other years their appearance has been delayed until May. Bevan also says, "the laying of drone eggs, which is called the great laying, usually commences at the end of April or the beginning of May." From the time of the egg being laid by the queen, to the time of the perfect insect leaving the cell, is exactly twenty-four days; by bearing this in mind, the time when the great laying takes place may easily be calculated in every apiary. We are disposed to think Dr. Bevan is correct in respect to the mass of drone-eggs being laid.

MASSACRE OF THE DRONES.

Many opinions prevail amongst bee-keepers as to the cause and manner in which drones are destroyed. It is well known that after the swarming, or rather when the honey-harvest begins to fail about the end of July or in August, a general massacre takes place. The first indication of this slaughter is casting out the baby drones to perish. Bevan remarks upon this subject—"The work of the drones being now completed, they are regarded as useless consumers of the fruits of others' labours, love is at once converted into hate, and a general proscription takes place. The unfortunate victims evidently perceive their danger, for they are never at this time seen resting in one place, but darting in and out of the hive with the utmost precipitation, as if in fear of being seized." Huber says he ascertained that the death of these insects was caused by the sting of the workers, whilst others have declared that they were harassed and driven from the hive by the more active workers; thus they are wearied of life. In some of our hives we have found on examination, before closing them up for the winter, the drones in a large mass dead in one corner of the hive. These must evidently have died of actual starvation, and we believe their death results more from starvation than any other cause, although we have seen others tumbled unceremoniously out of the hive, writhing in the throes of death on the ground. These were doubtless stung to death.

In other instances we have observed them crawling beneath the hive disabled by having their wings injured and bitten off. All these methods may be resorted to, to get rid of the useless members of the colony; but we think the bees never resort to the sting except when all other means have failed to effect their purpose (as this may cause also the death of the worker bee). It is curious to note that in some seasons the massacre will take place simultaneously in nearly all the hives in the apiary. Huber records an observation of this kind when six hives commenced the destruction on July 4, and with the same peculiarities in every case.

HOW LONG DO DRONES LIVE?

The drones in this country put in an appearance usually in the month of May. Some, it is true, are discovered in April; but we now speak of the great mass, or what some writers have called the general hatching.

Their average life will not be more than three months. If the colony has suffered the loss of their queen and is forced to raise another from the egg of a worker, then the hive defers the destruction of the drones. In cases of this kind they may be allowed to live four months. In some few instances we have discovered drones in the hive in the depth of winter, but never in a stock having a vigorous and fertile queen; it has been in hives devoid of a queen. Huber is said to have found them in his hive in January. We have *never* found them in prosperous hives, and it may be at once set down that something is going wrong if drones are seen so late in the season, and the sooner the hive is overhauled the better.

Drones die immediately after the

QUEEN'S WEDDING.

We do not know whether this statement has ever been satisfactorily solved; it is, however, generally believed. Neighbour in his excellent little manual thus writes:—
"The drone that happens to be the selected husband is by no means so fortunate as at first sight appears, for it is a law of Nature that the bridegroom does not survive the wedding-day. Her Majesty, although thus left a widow, is by no means a sorrowful bride, for she soon becomes the mother of a large family. It cannot be said that she pays no respect to the memory of her departed lord, for she never marries again. As is the case with most insects, the queen once impregnated continues productive during the remainder of her existence." Old queens, however, are said to lay none but drone-eggs.

HOW TO REGULATE OR KEEP DOWN THE DRONES.

Sometimes the stock is overfilled with these idle insects, who never gather a drop of honey. Even if they gathered sufficient for their own maintenance it would not appear so bad, but they are often produced in such enormous numbers that some plan must be adopted to keep them down, or the colony will suffer to that extent that it is useless to expect any surplus honey from it. In the barframe hives it is easy to take out the bars and cut out all the drone-cells, which ought to be done early in the season; but in common straw skeps or the Ayrshire hives it is exceedingly difficult to extract any of the drone-comb. Our continental apiarians, especially those in Germany, are always wide awake, and are continually inventing some new method, so as to make apiculture as *profitable* as possible.

We strongly recommend all our readers to adopt our simple and cheap Bar-frame Hives; but, as many of our village bee-farmers still persist in using the common straw hives, they will doubtless be glad to hear of the dronecatcher.

THE DRONE-CATCHER.

This is a simple though clever contrivance for entrapping these useless insects—one, moreover, which can be made by any working-man who is able to use his pocketknife, and knows how to twist a few wires. Without any description on our part, its construction may be gleaned from the engraving. It is a simple cage, the mouth being cut out of a block of wood, and the wires of the cage being large enough to allow the worker to escape, whilst, at the same time it imprisons the larger drone. It acts precisely upon the same principle as the "catch-em-alive" mouse-traps. The mouth and the bottom-board should, if possible, be made of one piece of timber, and a part should be cut off the mouth corresponding with the letter *a* to allow the workers returning from the fields to

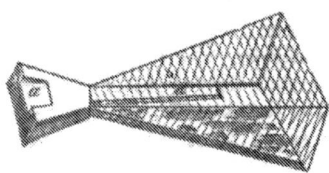

DRONE CAGE.

enter the hive. It is advisable when using this trap to place it on the hive about 2 o'clock in the afternoon, and to watch it, so that when filled it may at once be taken from the hive and emptied; thus the hive or worker bees will not be hindered in their work. We have seen them made with a loose mouth; these are far better to work, for the simple reason when the drones are killed with boiling water they may the more easily be taken from the trap. The part marked *a'* is a prolongation of the mouth; this is to prevent the drones crawling back to the hive again, which they would easily do if the wire-work was only connected with the hive. Those of our readers who have not the opportunity or inclination to make these traps may obtain them from Messrs. Neighbour, of High Holborn, London.

The use of the drone-trap saves the worker-bees much extra labour and some danger.

LIGURIAN, OR ITALIAN BEES.

Not a few authors have looked upon these beautiful insects as merely a novelty, a new toy or fashion, which, like fashions in dress, would rapidly change and disappear. We, however, think they are a most useful novelty, and a fashion which we trust will never again disappear from our English apiaries. As to their superiority, the following facts speak for themselves. They are a much larger bee, also very beautiful, although they are and can certainly be proved to be only a variety of the common black bee.

By very careful testing, side by side, with their older sisters, the queens are larger and more prolific. The workers are less sensitive to cold; and when bred in combs of their own building they are much larger, and as a natural result the honey sac is larger, thus they must be better honey gatherers. They also appear to be far better tempered; very rarely do they venture an attack. Dr. Kirtland remarks with truth, that their beauty of colouring and graceful forms render them an object of interest to every person of taste. My colonies are daily watched and admired by many visitors. They will, no doubt, prove a valuable acquisition to localities of high latitude, and will be peculiarly adapted to our climate. Langstroth declares, "If we may judge from the working of my colonies, the Italians will fully sustain their European reputation; they have gathered more than twice as much honey as the swarms of the common bee."

Quinby says, "I now began to watch their peculiarities with considerable interest. White clover was blossoming in abundance, and the early red, or June clover, in small quantities. Here was a chance to see if the Italians frequented the red clover more than the natives. I found nine Italians to two natives on this plant (the two exceptions might have been black hybrids). This was important to me; if the honey from white clover would sustain 60 or 80 colonies, that from the red would sustain nearly as many more, and I could keep double the number in each yard."

It has been asserted by several observers that they are longer lived. We cannot, from our limited observation, declare if this be so, but it would account for their swarming properties, which excel everything we have witnessed in native bees. They swarm more, begin some two or three weeks earlier, and continue later in the autumn. This may arise, in some measure, from their vigorous nature. Watch the hives some dull morning; here are two skeps, one containing pure Italians, the other black bees; the Italian whizzes past you with terrific force, whilst the black bees seem to go lazily along, as if it was too much trouble to go abroad on so dull a day. In rainy weather the Ligurians are as active as possible, when the black bees never stir out of the hives.

One season our Italians began to swarm three weeks before the others; the first we hived came out on 20th May, the second from the same hive on 30th May. By the 11th July the same hive again sent out a very large swarm. The first swarm, on 20th May, again swarmed on 7th July, a virgin swarm—very scarce with us, and another on 20th July; whilst the second swarm, hived 30th May, swarmed on 19th July, making a total of six swarms in one season; four of them were sold in the autumn for 8*l.* This same year, being a wretched honey season, my black bees could scarcely live; out of five hives we only obtained four swarms.

As honey-gatherers they far excel the others, and, if the bee-farmer do not keep the honey extractor constantly going, they will speedily fill the whole hive with honey to the exclusion of eggs, for no sooner does the sharp-eyed Ligurian observe a tenantless cell than it is speedily made use of for honey; but if the two end bars are removed frequently, and the honey taken out, it will prevent them encroaching upon the central combs, which will, in this case, be conscientiously used as a nursery.

THE VALUE OF ITALIANS.

To the active bee-farmer this bee opens up a rich harvest. Hundreds of bee-keepers would gratefully purchase swarms of pure Italians, but they cannot be obtained excepting at exorbitant prices, too high for the general run of bee-keepers in this country. A few words may help our readers to help themselves. First, if possible, and no other way seems open, purchase a queen from some dealer who will deal honestly with you, and introduce this to a good flourishing stock in the Bee-Farmer's Barframe Hive. Keep this stock apart from your other bees, at some cottage, where no bees are kept for some distance. Early the following year it will commence swarming. Take care of every hive or swarm until you have succeeded in obtaining a good apiary of Italians. The following year you may search for orders for swarms; each will be worth a guinea if sent away the same day as hived in a common skep; the honey of itself will reward your toils; this can be gleaned whilst the breeding and swarming are in active operation. Speaking within bounds, a second year should witness a dozen good swarms; we say this from experience. A working man, on the outskirts of Manchester, a few years ago, realised in one year 120*l.* from his Italian swarms. In a quiet neighbourhood sheltered from the winds vast results

THE VALUE OF ITALIANS.

should be obtained from the bee-farm, even with common bees, and much more with Ligurians.

To introduce an Italian queen the following method should be pursued:—Having smoked the native stock, remove the top board as gently as possible, because the queen is so shy and retiring that it is difficult to find her. Search each bar-frame separately, then remove them to an empty hive placed so as to be handy for use. If the search be unsuccessful over the frames, examine the clusters of bees in the corners of the hive. When found, remove her with care to a cage, together with a few workers, *i. e.* to a small box, in which a piece of comb, 3 × 2 inches, filled with honey, is placed. She may be wanted again, for it may unfortunately occur, as it did once to ourselves, that the strange queen is not accepted by the stock; in such a case the old queen by being replaced saves the entire stock.

When the queen is removed replace all the bars in the old hive, with the bees; the loss of the queen will not be detected immediately, but after the lapse of a few hours they will be discovered running to and fro eagerly searching for her amongst the combs.

Introduce the new queen thus: Secure her with two or three of the workers and a little honey in a wire cloth cage and insert it between the combs. This is to insure her safety. At the end of twenty-four hours or thereabouts she may be loosened on the top of one of the bars. She will then be welcomed by her new subjects.

We sometimes sprinkle a small quantity of syrup amongst the bees just before liberating the queen, or smoke the stock well from the entrance. We have never known a queen sacrificed when these simple precautions have been adopted.

HOW TO FILL THE APIARY WITH ITALIAN STOCKS.

We are not well versed in raising artificial queens, because we have never followed this method; our plan having been, to make the apiary profitable. An apiary in which experiments are being constantly performed will never prove successful. The late Rev. W. C. Cotton at one time purchased fourteen good stocks the same year, and lost them all by experiments. We, therefore, give Mr. Quinby's account of artificial rearing of Italian queens, so that any bee-farmer who wishes to do so may try his plan.

"Queens enough can be reared in one summer to supply the whole apiary no matter how many may be required, and if this is decided upon take no pains to isolate, but rear all the queens at home, and let them meet the native drone. These will produce *mixed workers* but pure drones.

"To rear queens artificially, inclose a few bees, a pint or a quart, without a queen, with a small piece of comb containing larvæ or eggs. To do this, make a little box or minature hive large enough to hold three combs or more—four or five inches square. Suspend frames within just as in the hive. Fit in them pieces of dry comb, and fasten with a bit of tin. Get a piece of comb containing eggs or larva (about two inches square); cut a piece exactly the same size, except underside, out of the middle of one of the combs and insert it. The bees will weld it fast in a few hours. Not finding a queen, they will in a few hours commence rearing one or more, by converting common cells into queen cells, and working larvæ into queens. When the larvæ are just the right age six or eight queens will sometimes be matured in ten or eleven days; at other times in sixteen or eighteen; but if the grub is over four days old it is doubtful if it can be changed to a queen.

"The bees to rear queens should, when practicable, be obtained from hives at least a mile and a half from the place where the queens are to be raised. Take them from a strong colony. If from the box-hive, invert it and drive out a quart or two into an empty hive or box; look out the queen if among them and put her back. If they are to be taken from the moveable comb hive, take out two or three combs and shake off the bees beside the box, into which they will run if it is set down with one edge raised a little, taking care all the time not to get the queen. If the bees have been taken from a colony at home it will be necessary to confine them from thirty-six to forty-eight hours, otherwise they may return to the old colony; but if the bees be taken in the middle of the day the majority will be young bees that have never left the hive, thus far more valuable for your purpose.

"From noon to 3 p.m. is decidedly the best time in the day to obtain the brood. Whilst busy at work the bees have not time to notice what is going on. Go to the hive containing your best Italian brood, and take out different combs till you find a brood of the right age, and with a sharp knife cut out suitable pieces. Care must be taken not to allow brood or queen cells to become chilled."

If several queens be raised at one time in the box they must be watched daily; the first hatched will ruthlessly destroy the others, if not prevented.

We have heard repeated and loud complaints from our neighbours that the yellow bees are dreadful thieves; there may be some truth in this statement. They will defend their own hives with a determined dogged perseverance to the death. No one need be alarmed lest the Italians be robbed, yet we fear they are themselves robbers when they have the chance, but it is always weak defenceless stocks that they plunder.

We advise our English bee-farmers to have none but *pure-bred* Ligurians; the half-breeds or hybrids are very savage in disposition, and are far from being so industrious; neither are they better as to swarming than our black bees.

BEES IN OTHER LANDS.

The continent of Africa in all its widely-extended regions seems well stocked with bees, particularly towards the sea-coast. In Lower Egypt their cultivation forms the employment of many of the poorer classes during a great part of the year. During the inundation of the Nile the cultivators, unable to find pasturage for their bee-stocks in the lower province, transport them in boats to Upper Egypt, resting occasionally by the way to allow the industrious insects an opportunity to forage. The insect supposed to be *Apis fasciata* bears a considerable resemblance to that cultivated in Greece. On the western coast, where it is intersected by the Senegal, separated as this region is from the most northerly parts of Africa by mountains and deserts which form an insuperable barrier to the passage of the inferior classes of animals, we find what we are assured is another species of bee, viz. *A. Adansonii*. It has, however, a very near resemblance to the Ligurian bee, its difference being in the first two rings of the abdomen, and the anterior half of the third, which are of a pale chestnut colour. In the neighbourhood of Gambia a species of small black bee is found in the woods, in all likelihood the same with those last mentioned; and the town of Vintain, situated on the southern side of the river, is much resorted to by Europeans on account of the great quantities of bees'-wax brought thither for sale. It is collected in the woods by the Feloops, a wild and unsociable race of people. The honey they chiefly use themselves in making a strong intoxicating liquor, much the same as the mead which is produced in this country. It is said by some writers that the bees along the west coast of Africa are destitute of stings. It was not so found by Park, to whom we are indebted for the above information; and that those further in the interior, about the eleventh degree of west longitude, are well provided with this formidable weapon appears from the following incident mentioned by the same traveller as having taken place near Doofroo: "We had no sooner unloaded the asses than some of our people, being in search of honey, unfortunately disturbed a large swarm of bees. They came out in immense numbers, and attacked men and beasts at the same time. Luckily most of the asses were loose, and galloped up the valley; but the horses and people were very much stung, and obliged to scamper off in all directions—in fact, for half-an-hour the bees seemed completely to have put an end to our journey. In the evening, when they became less troublesome and we could venture to collect our cattle, we found many of them much stung and swelled about the head. Three asses were missing; one died in the evening, and one next morning. Our guide lost his horse, and many of the people were much stung about the hands and face."

On the eastern side of the same continent the bees appear to resemble those of the western coast in their colour and diminutive size, but differ from them in the mode of constructing their nests, which are formed under the surface of the ground, while those of the others are lodged in the hollows of trees. To the southward and in the Hottentot countries the insects are found in great numbers, but, as appears from the report of some late travellers, never build their nests in the trunks of trees; and, though they are sometimes found nestling under the surface of the ground, make their dwellings chiefly in the clefts of the rocks; and one large rock in the Cape Colony has so long served as a favourite residence to these insects as to obtain from the Dutch settlers the name of Honig Kiss, *i.e.*, honey-rock. The following anecdotes relating to this species are from Burchel's *Travels in Africa* (vol. i. 377): "My bedding having been left out in the open air all day, we found in the evening the mattress taken possession of by a swarm of bees which had taken shelter under it for the night, and as a favour to these industrious creatures we left them undisturbed. They remained there till the next day at noon, when they departed in quest of some convenient chink in the rocks for their hive. Their manner of swarming appeared to us to differ in nothing from that of the common English bee. The same species, or others of the genus Apis, abounds in every part of this continent which has come under my observation, and is everywhere eagerly robbed of its honey. None of these nations have the least idea of bringing them under domestic management, but are content to take the honey wherever it is found; and this being done, often at an improper season, they make a useless destruction of the larvæ or young bees still in the cells." "One of the Hottentots observed a number of bees entering a hole in the ground which had formerly belonged to some animal of the weasel kind. As he made signs for us to come to him, we turned that way fearing he had met with some accident; and, when the people began to unearth the bees, I did not expect that we should escape without being severely stung. But they knew so well how to manage an affair of this kind, that they robbed the poor insects with the greatest ease and safety. Before they commenced digging a fire was made near the hole,

BEES IN OTHER LANDS. 137

and constantly supplied with damp fuel to produce a cloud of smoke. In this the workman was completely enveloped; so that the bees returning from the fields were prevented from approaching, and those which flew out of the nest were driven by it to a distance. Yet the rest of our party to avoid their resentment found it prudent either to ride off or stand also in the smoke. About three pounds of honey were obtained, which, excepting a small share which I reserved till tea-time, they instantly devoured in the comb; and some of the Hottentots professed to be equally fond of the larvæ. The honey appeared unusually limpid, and nearly as thin as water, yet it seemed as sweet and of as delicate a taste as the best honey of England.

"Whilst I was engaged in the chase one day on foot with a Namaqua attendant, he picked up a small stone, looked at it earnestly, then over the plain, and threw it down again. I asked what it was, he said there was the mark (excrement) of a bee on it; taking it up, I also saw upon it a small pointed drop of wax, which had fallen from the bee in its flight. The Namaqua noticed the direction the point of the drop indicated, and, walking on, he picked up another stone, also with a drop of wax on it, and so on at considerable intervals, till, getting behind a crag, he looked up, and bees were seen flying across the sky, and in and out of a cleft in the face of the rock. Here, of course, was the honey he was in pursuit of. A dry bush is selected, fire is made, the cliff is ascended, and the nest is robbed in the smoke."

African travellers give us an amusing account of one of the modes by which the natives of the interior are enabled to discover the spot where the bees have deposited their treasures. They are guided by a small bird (*Cuculus Indicus*) of a brownish-grey colour, well named the honey-guide. This little creature is very fond of honey and bee-bread; but, unable by its own exertions to gratify its taste, it directs the negroes by a peculiar cry or whistle to the tree where the bees have taken up their residence, advancing before them by longer or shorter flights, according to the greater or lesser distance of the object of pursuit. If its followers lag behind, it returns with manifest impatience, and by its redoubled cries appears to chide their delay. As it approaches the tree, its flights become more limited, its whistle is repeated at shorter intervals, and at last, having brought its associates to the desired spot, it hovers over it for a moment, as if to mark it out distinctly, and then quietly takes up a station at a little distance, waiting the result, and expecting its share of the booty, which it never fails to obtain.

In the island of Madagascar and the Mauritius is to be found the single coloured bee (*Apis unicolor*) of a bright shining black, without spots or coloured bands. Its honey, as appears by a specimen brought home by a French vessel, is highly aromatic, and is, while in the cells, or when recently abstracted, of a green colour, but becomes afterwards of a reddish-yellow. In these islands the bee is domesticated, and a French naturalist, M. de Lanux, has published a memoir on the form of the Madagascar hives, a circumstance which naturally leads to the supposition that the inhabitants pay considerable attention to the cultivation of this insect.

Knox, in his History of Ceylon, enumerates three kinds of bees found in that island; the first of which bears a close resemblance to the European insect, though it would seem by no means so irritable, and, like those near the Cape of Good Hope, builds in hollow trees, and also in holes in the ground which have been made by some burrowing animals. The natives, to obtain the honey, have merely to blow into these holes, upon which the bees instantly decamp without resistance, and the plunderers, without making use of any defensive covering, pull out the

combs with their hands, and deposit them in vessels brought
for that purpose. It is probable, from this account of
the facility with which this species is deprived of its stores,
and the fearlessness of the plunderers, that, like others to
be afterwards mentioned, it has no sting. A second species
found here is of a larger size and brighter colour than our
domestic bee. These build their nests in the branches of
trees, and generally at a great height. At a certain period
of the year the inhabitants of the towns go out in a body to
despoil them, and return laden with the booty. The third
species is a remarkably small bee, not larger than a common
fly, and of a blackish hue. Their honey is not generally
much regarded; but the children sometimes amuse themselves by cutting a hole in the trunk of the tree where it
is deposited, and carrying it off. Knox tells us that the
inhabitants not only devour the honey but have a strong
taste—akin to that of the Hottentots who feed on the
larvæ—for the bees themselves; and that when they discover a swarm on an inaccessible branch of a tree, they
stupify them with the smoke of torches, causing them to
drop on the ground, when they gather them and carry
them home, "boiling and eating them, and esteeming them
excellent food."

Honey bees abound also in the whole of the Eastern
Archipelago; but we have no certain account of their
distinctive characters. We only know that they generally
build on the boughs of trees, and that they are never
domesticated or collected into hives. In fact, no attention
is paid to them, further than what is requisite to obtain
their wax. This we are told (Marsden's *Sumatra*) is an
article of considerable importance in all the eastern islands,
from whence it is imported in large oblong cakes to China,
Bengal, and other parts of the continent. Their honey is
much inferior to that of Europe, as might be expected

from the nature of the vegetation. The honey of the *Apis Peronii*, found in the island of Timor, may be considered an exception to this. For our knowledge of this we are indebted to M. Peron, the intrepid French navigator, who describes it as having a yellowish tinge, more liquid than ours, and of an exquisite flavour. It is called by the natives bee-sugar. The distinctive characters of the insect itself consist of the two first rings of the abdomen (with the exception of their posterior edges), the base of the third, and the greater part of the breast, being of a reddish yellow, and the superior wings of a brownish hue. It appears, from recent accounts, that in the distant regions of New South Wales and Van Diemen's Land, besides the indigenous insect, the bee of Europe has obtained a firm footing, and already rivals the prolific race of South Carolina. The following account is from a periodical of extensive circulation and great utility (*Loudon's Magazine*). " The native bee is without a sting, and is not much larger than a common house-fly. It produces abundance of honey and wax, but has not yet been subjected to cultivation; and from its small size, and its building in very high trees, probably never will be so. The European bee has been oftener than once introduced into Sydney, but without success; the swarms having left the hive for the woods. A hive was carried to Van Diemen's Land, in the autumn of the year 1830, by Dr. T. B. Wilson, at the suggestion of his friend Mr. R. Gunter, of Earl's Court, brought from London in a wire case. It arrived in safety, and the bees swarmed several times the first year; and in the *True Colonist* (a Hobart Town newspaper) of Feb. 14th, 1835, it is stated that a hive descended from Dr. Wilson's, belonging to a gentleman in the neighbourhood of Hobart Town, had already swarmed eighteen times."

The most famous honey of antiquity was that of the bees of the Hymettus, near Athens. Of its deterioration a modern writer gives the following account:—

"This spot was certainly at one time more abundantly supplied with flowers than at present, these too so strongly scented that hounds on that account frequently lost trace of the game when hunting in these regions. But there is no land like Greece, in which for centuries the works not only of men but of nature also have been, as far as possible, destroyed. Trees and shrubs were cut down in the continued wars without any thought of the consequence, and what the axe spared the shepherds burned, in order to raise from the ashes, during the first year, a few blades of grass for their goats. Were not the Grecian climate so favourable the greater part of the country must long since have become a bare, stony, and rocky wilderness. The Hymettus has now no better vegetation than the mountains of Attica. The honey of the Laurion mountains was much prized (*Erica Mediterranea*, or tree heath, grows there in abundance). Throughout Greece honey is more agreeable and aromatic than in other lands, owing to the heat being moderate, for which reason the juices of the plants are in a more agreeably concentrated state.

"The honey of the Hymettus no longer possesses its superiority; it is in other neighbourhoods finer and more aromatic, *e. g.* in many of the Cyclades, especially in Siekino. The greatest quantity of honey is obtained from the monastery of Syrian, to the north-east of the city: it is delivered to the local archbishop. The shepherds at other parts of the Hymettus probably keep bee-hives, and the honey from Pentelicon is also reckoned among the Hymettic. The number of hives in these mountains yielding honey has been averaged of late years at five thousand. The principal food of these bees is *Satureja capitata*, then *Lentiscus*, rock-roses, sage, lavender, and other herbs.

Otherwise the Hymettus is very bare on its declivities, and in some of the dales are wild olives, with shrubs of myrtle, laurel, and oleander. The sea-pine grows on its summit very imperfectly, but near the monastery it is pretty. Besides this, can be found hyacinths, amaryllis lutea, dark violet crocus, &c., from all of which the bees extract their sweets."

SAGACITY OF BEES.

We adopt the word "sagacity" in preference to the word "instinct" as expressing our meaning more clearly.

The following facts may be familiar to some of our readers, still we may be excused for bringing them before them.

We have already cited the instance of a slug having entered a hive and been stung to death by the bees, after which, being unable to dislodge it, they covered it all over with propolis.

Bevan states, "A very striking illustration of the reasoning power of bees occurred to my friend Mr. Walrond. Inspecting his bee-boxes at the end of October, 1817, he perceived that a centre comb burthened with honey had separated from its attachment, and was leaning against another comb, so as to prevent the passage of the bees between them. This accident excited great activity in the colony, but its nature could not be ascertained at the time. At the end of a week, the weather being cold, and the bees clustered together, Mr. W. observed through the window of the box that they had constructed two horizontal pillars between the combs alluded to, and had removed so much of the honey and wax from the top of each as to allow the passage of a bee; in about ten days more, there was an uninterrupted

SAGACITY OF BEES.

thoroughfare; the detached comb at its upper part had been secured by a strong barrier and fastened to the window with the spare wax. This being accomplished, the bees removed the horizontal pillars first constructed as being of no further use. During this laborious process, (says Mr. W.) the glass window in the box was quite as warm as I had felt it during any part of the summer, and the bees were as active within the box."

We have ourselves witnessed a similar proceeding.

Huber has written a long chapter about his bees erecting barricades before the entrance of the hives, to defend the colony from the ravages of the sphinx-moth: this is certainly very interesting, and well worthy of much closer study. We do not, however, attribute *reason* to bees as several writers do.

Darwin's bold view will be remembered by many. " If we were better acquainted with those insects that are formed into societies—as the bees, wasps, and ants—we should find that their arts and improvements are not so similar and uniform as they now appear to us, but that they arose in the same manner (from experience and tradition) as the arts of our own species, though their reasoning is from few ideas, is busied about fewer objects, and is exerted with less energy."

SENSES OF BEES.

Bees have the sense of *smell* acutely developed; they can at once detect anyone covered with perspiration, and soon become angry if annoyed with offensive odours. An experiment made by Huber demonstrates their faculty of smell; he placed vessels of honey in boxes perforated with very small holes to allow the odour to escape, but not of sufficient size to permit a sight of the honey; the bees came directly to the boxes. He also tried this experiment by means of small card valves, which the bees, after examining the boxes all round, contrived to raise up that they might reach the honey. The extreme sensitiveness of smell is evinced by their promptitude in resenting an injury inflicted on any of their community: thus, if any of the bees are crushed in hiving a swarm, it makes them angry. This experiment may be tried: present the sting, with its accompanying poison-bag, at the entrance of a hive, their enmity is immediately aroused. Woe to the bee-master, if he happens to be close at hand.

In reference to offensive breath, M. Hofer had been an admirer of bees many years, so that he would take the hive into the house and carry away the queen in presence of his friends; but he was attacked with a fever; on his recovery he again attempted this familiarity; the bees would never again allow of his approaching the hive, but fiercely resented it.

The sense of *touch* is also apparent; it is by this means, so it is supposed, they are enabled to carry on their operations in the darkness of the hive. The antennæ are thought to be employed for this purpose; we believe they have the sense of sound produced by these organs. Linnæus long believed that insects did not possess the sense of *hearing*; however, there cannot be the least doubt that bees have it acutely developed, for, according to *Huber*, they are keenly sensitive to the queen's song. But this does not need any argument; every bee-keeper who has been accustomed to drive bees knows that they quickly detect the drumming noise on their skep or hive, and become so terrified that in fifteen minutes almost every bee will have deserted the rich stores.

We cannot doubt also that *taste* is highly developed in the hive-bee. The tongue must have a wonderful power to detect so rapidly the different taste of nectar, so as to reject a flower with disdain, and immediately dash away to a more favourite blossom.

Eye-sight is said to be very imperfect in this insect. Dr. Dereham proves very beautifully that, the cornea and optic nerve being at one and the same distance, they are not fitted to observe objects close at hand but can see well at a little distance. This is a wise provision for so tiny an insect, enabling her to roam some miles away from her home. We frequently (remarks Dr. Evans) observe bees flying straight homewards, through the trackless air, as if in full view of the hive, then running their heads against it and seeming to feel their way to the door with their antennæ as if totally blind.

It may be suggested that they find their way home, when foraging at some distance, by the aid of memory; no one, however, who has carefully watched them, will deny that they fly in a *direct line*—" bee line," as it is called by the American honey-hunters.

On all these difficult problems we advise our readers who desire further information to study Langstroth We cannot conclude this short chapter without noticing the theory of Dr. Virey. He has given it as his opinion that there are seven senses, which he thus divides: Four physical, namely—touch, taste, smell, and love: Three intellectual, namely—hearing, sight, and thought. Whether love and thought should be added to the above enumeration of the acute senses of bees is rather questionable. We do not know upon what grounds their physical love has been made out, unless it has reference to the queen's wedding. Something resembling *thought* is very conspicuous in many of their operations, but it cannot be distinctly pronounced to be such without much more evidence than we now possess.

FOREIGN BEES.

Mr. Cotton in his *Bee-Book* has the following remarks on bees in Siberia:—

"Although these insects do sufficiently secure to man the fruit of their labours by that admirable form of government and polity which they observe amongst themselves, yet they are so formed by nature to serve him, whenever he shall see fit to employ them, as to be subject to his directions, and to fly obedient to his call in as orderly a manner as sheep obey the voice of their shepherd. As the herdsman, by the winding of his horn, draws forth horses, mules, goats, &c., from their stalls, and by a second signal leads them to the water, and by a third reconducts them home, in like manner the master of the hives by a blast of his whistle can call all the bees of the village after him, conducting them by this signal sometimes into one field of flowers, sometimes into another, thus taking them by turns, in order to give the flowers time to recruit their stock of sweets, and thereby afford the bees a fresh repast. With another blast of his whistle he leads them back to their hives, when either impending rains or the approach of night gives warning to sound a retreat.

"This was a very common as well as an ancient practice in the East, and to this the prophet Isaiah alludes when comparing the enemies which God brings upon any nation to afflict it to a swarm of bees which a shepherd calls or dismisses by a signal given. He says: 'The Lord shall hiss for the fly that is in the uttermost parts of the rivers of Egypt, and for the bee that is in the land of Assyria.' This custom existed in Asia in the fourth and fifth centuries, and St. Cyril speaks of it as a thing very common in his time, and which he had very often seen."

FOREIGN BEES.

Mr. Stedman in his work on Surinam relates the following characteristic anecdote about bees:—

"On the 16th I was visited by a neighbouring gentleman, whom I conducted up my ladder; but he had no sooner entered my aerial dwelling than he leaped down from the top to the ground, roaring like a madman with agony, after which he instantly plunged his head into the river; but, looking up, I soon discovered the cause of his distress to be an immense nest of wild bees, or wassee, in the thatch directly above my head, as I stood within my door; when I immediately took to my heels as he had done, and ordered them to be destroyed by my slaves without delay. A tar mop was now brought and the devastation just going to commence, when an old negro stepped up, and offered to receive any punishment I should decree if even one of these bees should sting me in person. 'Massa,' said he, 'they would have stung you long ere now had you been a stranger to them; but they being your tenants, that is, gradually allowed to build upon your premises, they assuredly know both you and yours, and will never hurt either you or them.' I instantly assented to the proposition, and, tying the old man to a tree, ordered my boy Quaco to ascend the ladder quite naked, which he did, and was not stung. I then ventured to follow, and declare, upon my honour, that even after shaking the nest, which made the inhabitants buzz about my ears, not a single one attempted to sting me. I next released the old negro, and rewarded him with a gallon of rum and four shillings for the discovery. This swarm of bees I kept unhurt, as my body guard, and they have made many overseers take a desperate leap for my amusement, as I generally sent them up my ladder upon some frivolous message, when I wished to punish them for injustice and cruelty, which was not seldom.

"The above negro assured me that on his master's estate was a tree, in which had been lodged ever since he could remember a society of birds, and another of bees, who lived in the greatest harmony together; but, should any strange bird come to feed on the bees, they were instantly repulsed by their feathered allies; and, if strange bees dared to venture near the birds' nests, the native swarm attacked the invaders, and stung them to death; that his master and family had so much respect for the above association that the tree was considered as sacred, and was not to be touched by an axe until it should yield to all-destroying time."

Basil Hall gives the following curious account of bees in South America:—

"From the Plaza we went to a house where a bee-hive of the country was opened in our presence. The bees, the honey-comb, and the hive differ essentially from those of Europe. The hive is generally made out of a log of wood from two to three feet long and eight or ten inches in diameter, hollowed out and closed at the end by circular doors cemented close to the wood, but capable of being removed at pleasure. Some persons use cylindrical hives, made of earthenware, instead of the clumsy apparatus of wood; these are relieved by raised figures and circular rings, so as to form rather handsome ornaments in the verandah of a house, where they are suspended by cords from the roof, in the same manner that the wooden ones in the villages are hung to the eaves of the cottages. On one side of the hive, half-way between the ends, there is a small hole made just large enough for a loaded bee to enter, and shaded by a projection to prevent the rain from trickling in. In this hole, generally representing the mouth of a man, or some monster, the head of which is moulded in the clay of the hive, a bee is constantly stationed, whose office is no sinecure, for the hole is so small that he has to draw back every time a bee wishes to enter or leave the hive. A gentleman told me that an experiment had been made of marking the sentinel, when it was observed the same bee continued at his post all day.

"When it is ascertained by the weight that the hive is full, the end pieces are removed, and the honey withdrawn. The hive we saw opened was only partly filled, which enabled us to see the economy of the interior to more advantage. The honey is not contained in the elegant hexagonal cells of our hives; but in wax bags not quite so large as an egg. These bags, or bladders, are hung round the sides of the hive, and appear about half full, the quantity probably being just as great as the strength of the wax will bear without tearing; those nearer the bottom, being better supported, are more filled than the upper ones. In the centre or lower part of the hive we observed an irregular-shaped mass of comb, furnished with cells like those of our bees, all containing young ones, in such an advanced state that when we broke the comb and let them out they flew merrily away. During this examination of the hive, the comb and the honey were taken out, and the bees disturbed in every way, but they never stung us, though our faces and hands were covered with them. It is said, however, that there is a bee in this country which does sting, but the kind that we saw seemed to have neither the inclination nor the power, for they certainly did not hurt us, and our friends said, they were *muy manso*, or very tame, and never stung any one. The honey gave out a rich aromatic perfume, and tasted differently from ours, but possessed an agreeable flavour."

FOUL-BROOD.

I have seen the effects of that fearful disease, the rinderpest, amongst our live-stock, and never witnessed one clear case where an animal was attacked and showed unmistakable signs of the disease in which it recovered. We have also heard heartrending accounts of the cholera, and, what was even worse, the dreadful plague of London. Bad though all these were, yet in their desolating effects they are as nothing compared with the foul-brood amongst bees. Some of our readers may smile at my making this comparison, and may even think foul-brood is made too much of by scientific apiarians, but, if they witnessed its frightful ravages when it makes its appearance in an apiary, they would be, as I have been, amazed at its effects. I write, not as most of our authors and writers upon this subject, merely to describe the disease, but I speak from experience. I have observed it as introduced into an apiary of fifteen fine stocks, kept by a medical man, who prided himself upon his advanced system of management, and had the most improved Woodbury hives and other appliances: in this instance it was brought in with an Italian queen, and, though everything was adopted on scientific bases to check the disease, all was in vain. In one season every stock was infected, and by the autumn my friend had not a single stock living—they were all dead. Had the disease not spread, the matter would not have been so serious, but in one season almost every stock throughout the whole neighbourhood—and some were nearly half a mile apart—was diseased and worthless. This will to some extent show its frightfully infectious nature, and the fearful rapidity with which the infection spreads.

Dzierzon, the celebrated scientific apiarian of Germany, commenced about 1838 with a single stock, but these had so wonderfully increased that in the year 1848 he prided himself upon having more than 500 stocks. In the interval he had lost seventy colonies from thieves, sixty destroyed by fire, and twenty-four by a flood. In the year 1848, he states, "a fearful pestilence made its appearance in my apiary, which spread so fast that it contaminated every stock and artificial swarm I then possessed." He lost this year more than 500 stocks from the foul-brood. This was almost enough to dishearten any man, and make him resolve never to keep bees again.

It made its appearance amongst my stocks in 1870. At first I could not tell what was amiss, for the bees became quite dispirited. If any were seen working it was only with a lazy kind of effort, which seemed to indicate disease. I then removed those which were infected to a distance of nearly three miles, thinking it was possible to save them, but I had my trouble for nothing, for they gradually dwindled away, until before the autumn all became so weak that I buried both hives and bees to stay the spread of the disease. I find from experiments that if a healthy colony is fed with honey from a diseased stock they will be quickly infected; also, the disease is spread more by robbing than all other causes combined. When a stock is weak the neighbouring colonies, as well as those at a distance of a mile or so around, will prey upon it; but if a few bees from an infected stock are placed in a healthy hive they seem to carry the infection with them, although they are strong and healthy; but we must bear in mind that it is the young brood in the cells which become diseased and putrefy, and not the old bees. Some authors have proposed to remove the queen; supposing that, breeding being thus prevented, the disease could not spread from hive to hive. The better plan is to destroy the stock if they are diseased. It is a hopeless task to attempt to cure them by any means; they only make matters worse if kept on the stand.

Can nothing be done to stay its ravages? Nothing has yet had any influence in this direction, for chemicals, &c., all seem to be powerless. We must not forget that the disease infects the brood in the cells, and induces putrefaction, thus causing a most intolerable stench to issue from the diseased stock. The cells are filled with a dark-coloured, half liquid mass, resembling treacle.

Many causes have been assigned for this disease. Some talented and thoughtful bee-keepers have supposed it was caused at first by the brood being chilled; thus dying, they decay in the cells, and become a putrefying mass. This theory has long since disappeared. Microscopical science has revealed the true secret, which is a kind of mould (*fungus*), the spores from which may float about in the atmosphere, and when they find a suitable nidus they speedily generate the foul-brood so called.

Speaking from my limited experience of this fearful malady as it appeared in North of England apiaries, I cannot hold out any hopes of a successful remedy. Where the bees are in straw skeps it is wise to destroy the stock, of course saving both honey and wax, for these are in no case injured for domestic consumption; then either burn the hive, or destroy it in some way, for to use it again without disinfection is only to foster the disease. But where wooden hives are employed in the apiary I should advise the bee-keeper to boil them well in soda, then disinfect them thoroughly by means of either carbolic acid or chloride of lime. Never allow any of your healthy stocks to feed on honey taken from a diseased stock; some of my friends have thought they could do no harm by so doing, until, when too late, they discovered their folly.

The appearance of the foul-brood, or of a stock thus infected, is a thoroughly disheartening sight; they seem to have no energy or wish to labour—they fly about in a lazy kind of manner, and linger much about the entrance. Inside is worse still; the cells, generally sealed over, may be detected at once by having a dark colour, and with a few holes in each: every cell-cover is sunken. I hope none of my readers may have the sad experience of this infectious disease that I have had. It is enough, especially in the case of a young apiarian, to compel him to give up the pursuit in disgust, after labouring hard to make the apiary profitable; besides, the expense incident to all enterprises of the kind is far from trivial, and then to find all in vain—nothing but loss—is very disheartening. My advice to everybody is simply this: Take care, in the first instance, to secure your first stocks from a healthy apiary, and do not employ or use any foreign honey in feeding your colonies—syrup, after all, is the best and most reliable food; and be careful in introducing any new queens.

THE ENEMIES OF OUR HONEY-BEE.

The domestic honey-bee has many enemies to contend against of one kind or other; man and beasts, insects and reptiles, together with birds, are all sworn enemies to the industrious, toiling bees, but the worst enemy of all is man. Other foes may destroy great numbers of bees, and rob them of an immense quantity of honey, but he slays at once the whole colony. Other enemies may take a pound or so of honey, but he is so greedy and selfish as to take the whole contents of the hive. I cannot do better to illustrate this part of my subject than quote the words of a recent writer upon this theme: "Finally, the worst enemy of bees is man. There is the barbarous, cruel, and ungrateful treatment of the brimstone-match. The little innocents have toiled all the summer. They have thrown off a swarm—after the example of the Church of Scotland, which, by way of showing its internal strength, threw off a capital swarm in 1843—they have recovered all the effects of their secession, and amassed abundance for future days. The bee-cide felon called man digs a pit, lights four ounces of brimstone inside of it, and deliberately sets fifteen thousand bees, queen and all, above its really and truly infernal fumes,—suffocates and burns the unhappy martyrs, and then subscribes to various charities, and calls himself a philanthropist!!! He ought to be sent to the treadmill. Why does the Society for Preventing Cruelty to Animals take up the case of cab-horses, and overlook the murdered bees? But there are regular inquisitors who do not use sulphur. These scientific crinkum-crankum hives, from which bees with difficulty get out and with more difficulty get in, are little purgatories, over which the inquisitors preside. Vivisection is no worse. Yet these men complain that all who advocate simple, easily accessible, and comfortable homes for bees, are behind the age, and ignorant of apiarian progress. Do not let your bees find by painful experience that their bee-master is their worst enemy." Thus, without any explanation on my part, it will clearly be seen that man is the chief enemy of our domestic honey-bee—often, may be, from sheer ignorance of their requirements and habits. But he is not the sole enemy; he may be the only biped foe, yet there are other foes to be dreaded among the quadrupeds: for example, the fox, bear, rats, and mice. We do not so much fear any depredation in our day from the fox, and it seems superfluous to class it amongst the bee-enemies so far as England is concerned. In other countries, however, they are formidable foes, as, for instance, in France, where, if report is to be credited, he relishes a morsel of honey-comb, and passes by the hen-roost, perhaps filled with choice turkeys and fat geese, to overturn the bee-hives. On the other hand, in this country he seems to disregard either the bees or bee-hives. M. Ducarne says: "These rascals of foxes eat the bees as well as the honey, but it is the honey to which they are most partial. For two years a particular fox came every winter to overthrow my hives. I put a chicken and some bread to amuse him, and some poison to kill him; but no, the cunning thief would not touch either, he went directly to the hives. Mark the sagacity of the animal; he would not come in the summer, when the bees were in full vigour, as he knew in what manner he would be received, but he steals slily to the hives when the inhabitants are in a state of torpor, and thus obtains their treasure without incurring any danger himself."

Another enemy we need not fear, in our day at all events, is the bear. He doubtless loves honey, and proves himself a capital bee-hunter in the primeval forests of the far-west of America. When a bee-tree is discovered, he will gnaw at the hollow trunk for several days, until he has made a hole sufficiently large to admit his enormous paws; then he pulls out in one confused mass honey, bee-bread, wax, and bees, and leisurely enjoys his feast. No wonder he is fat, when he retires to some secure place, generally a hollow elm-tree, lined most luxuriously with dried grass and leaves in the autumn, and lies in a torpid state until awakened by the warmth of the following spring. The Abbé del Rocca mentions some singular traits of sagacity regarding this animal. It appears the bear seldom attacks a hive openly, for fear of the stings, but he will in a most gentle manner take the hive in his paws and carry it out to the first river or pond, in which he plunges it until all the bees are drowned. The bee-keepers in those regions in which the bear abounds, knowing his sly sagacity, chain down their hives to the stand, or fasten them securely to walls and tree-trunks, so that the bear, unable to carry them away, will not molest them, except in the autumn, when the bees are less active.

Coming near home, rats and mice are undoubted enemies of the honey-bee. When the bees are removed to the shelter of a dry shed or outhouse, for the winter, they should be frequently examined. In the summer months it is but seldom that either rats or mice will venture to attack a vigorous colony, from the simple fact that they would be roughly handled and rudely repulsed if they attempted an entrance. In the case of mice it is doubtful if they would escape with their lives. In the winter, however, matters are reversed, and mice especially will often, if the bees happen to be on a low bee-bench, find a shelter in the hive, where they find such snug warm quarters. They then speedily set to work, after having eaten a hole in the combs sufficiently large to construct a nest of hay or straw. Rats cannot effect an entrance through the mouth of the hive, but when reduced to straits in cold weather, if they can meet with old straw skeps, they are not long in making an entrance for themselves. There is this difference betwixt mice and rats, when regarded as bee-enemies: mice eat the bees. Judging of a few cases in my personal experience, they must consume a large quantity, from the number of heads and wings found on and around the stand. Rats on the contrary take little notice of the bees, but consume the honey. In a few days a single rat will eat up the whole of the winter store. Destroy them if you can, the sooner the better, and thus save your bees from this plague. Darwin makes it out very satisfactorily that if the cats increase mice must as a result decrease, and humble-bees rapidly increase; as a consequence, the favourite pansy of our gardens will produce an abundant crop of fertile seeds. The pansy or heartease cannot be fertilised without insect agency. Its fertilization is mostly performed by humble-bees. The greatest enemy the humble-bees perhaps have to contend against is mice. If cats are scarce, mice, of course, increase, and thus you must in a short time, unless the balance of nature is kept up, lose the much-loved pansy. Mice are doubly hateful to the bees; they create a most disagreeable stench where they find a lodging, so much so that the bees on the return of spring will not be long in seeking a new home, and in abandoning the old tenement to the mice. Sometimes the losses by this

THE ENEMIES OF OUR HONEY-BEE.

means entailed upon bee-keepers in some parts of England are very heavy. The best plan to free the bees from the depredations of this animal is to place the hives on single pedestals, or stands, about two feet high, and as winter approaches lessen the entrance, so that only two bees can pass and repass at each time. Espinasse says he has known mice to take up their residence in hives without destroying the bees. This is contrary to the experience of every practical apiarian with whom I have come in contact. Mice are unable to walk in a reverted direction; therefore hives on simple single stands are secure, unless something is placed against them, as is frequently done from thoughtlessness; then these creatures, ever on the watch for an opportunity, ascend. I have often thought that they are tempted to enter straw hives because of their resemblance in miniature to stacks of hay or straw, for they are never known to enter wooden hives, and it is morally certain they cannot smell either honey or bees in cold weather; thus they are probably allured at first by the thought of feasting on grain, such as wheat or oats, then, finding something more sweet, they speedily become tenants at will.

Huish recommends a trap of the following construction to destroy them, if they are lurking anywhere in the neighbourhood of the apiary:—"Let a pea be soaked in water, then draw a thread through it, and tying a small stick at each end, place it in the ground the exact distance of the width of a brick; the brick is then placed on the thread, and the mouse coming to gnaw the pea gnaws also the thread, and, the support of the brick being thus taken away, it falls and kills the mouse." This kind of trap may be found very serviceable, as mice are remarkably fond of seed-peas. Sparrows are blamed for much of the damage done to the rows of seed-peas in our gardens in early spring, whereas it is nearly, if not all, done by mice. Would not the common spring wire-trap, baited with oatmeal, answer much better than the one advocated by Huish?

The toad may be considered as a great devourer of bees, and he does it in a very cruel and wicked manner. He gets close beneath the stand, amongst weeds or behind some heaps of earth, with just his head only peeping out, and, being almost the colour of dry earth, it is difficult to detect his presence. In summer, just before swarming, when the evenings are warm, the bees cluster outside like a large bunch of grapes, often hanging from beneath the stand for five or six inches. Now and then, two or three bees will by some accident be loosened from the cluster, and drop on the ground. No sooner does this happen than they are gobbled up by the reptile; thus the poor bees have but little chance to defend themselves. Again, a toiling industrious worker has been out on the heath, perhaps some miles away from home, when it returns laden with both honey and pollen. Weary and exhausted when it arrives at home, just as it reaches the alighting board it drops off and falls. The toad on the watch snatches it up in his ugly maw, and it is seen no more. The toad not only watches for bees, but is frequently seen close by the wall or hedge-bank which harbours a wasp's nest, and as greedily devours these yellow gentry as he does the more sober-tinted bees.

The only safeguard against this foe is to watch for his appearance. When he sits " seeking whom he may devour" in the eventide, take him by the hind leg and throw him as far as possible over the fence. It will take him some days, probably, before he will be able to reach his old quarters. In some of our popular bee-books I have seen the recommendation to empty the snuff-box on his back. This is great cruelty, and cannot be used, even on a toad, with a clear conscience. Our Irish bee-keepers, through the kindness of their patron saint, are fortunately delivered from this odious pest.

Without doubt, bees can reckon amongst their enemies the various kinds of soft-billed or insectivorous birds. The warblers probably destroy many bees, but the worst of this class of enemies is, that we are seldom able to detect them actually destroying bees, therefore we cannot often honestly charge them with this hideous crime. Very few birds venture so close to our dwellings, as the bench which supports the cottage hives is situated no further away than beneath the kitchen window. Thousands, we believe, of our honey-bees are picked off the blossoms by birds, when, unsuspicious of danger, they are engaged sucking up the honey from the nectary of the flower. My bees are kept some distance away from my dwelling, therefore I have had a very good opportunity of watching closely this class of foes. After careful scrutiny I have come to this conclusion: that most of our birds which have been charged with this crime are innocent, in so far as killing the living insect is concerned. I have seen the thrush, tom-tit, robin readbreast, with several more, busy picking up for food the dead bees lying on the ground, beneath the stands, but I cannot say that I have ever seen them standing on either the hive or pedestal to catch the bees as they were leaving or returning to the hive.

The worst bird enemy the British apiarian has to contend against is, I am convinced, the fly-catcher. These birds may be seen, on calm summer evenings, flying to and fro, opposite the hives, and catching the poor bees on the wing. Yet this bird may, after all, do far more good than harm, in ridding the air of millions of insect pests. The atmosphere would be unbearable were it not for insectivorous birds. Not only so, what would become of our garden vegetables, fruits, &c. were it not for birds? It is astonishing the quantity of insects and worms a single pair of fly-catchers destroy in the length of a day. Each bird in the early part of the day will return to its nest, carrying chiefly a mouthful of insects for its unfledged young, not less than twenty times in an hour. This can scarcely be credited by some persons, yet "seeing is believing."

The lively little tom-tit has again and again been charged as a bee-murderer. Doubtless there is some truth in the charge, for Lapoutre, a French naturalist, says,— " I saw under a tree, in which there was a tom-tit's nest, a surprising quantity of the scaly parts of bees, which this bird had dropped from the nest." I scarcely, however, believe what Buffon places on record. In one of his works it is stated, " with its beak and claws it provokes the bees to come out, and then immediately seizes them." I have seen it on several occasions about the hives, going beneath the pedestal and poking its nose in every nook and corner that it could detect, but I feel assured it was only to pick up as food spiders and other insects, for the bees at the time were going to and fro in hundreds, yet it never molested them; this to me was sufficient proof that he has often been unjustly charged. I was much pleased with a letter in *The Times* some years ago, and my readers will, no doubt, pardon its reproduction:—

" Sir,—In reference to your interesting letters on bees, in *The Times* of last Thursday, I take leave to explain to you how I prevent tom-tits and other birds from molesting my industrious little friends, if they should feel so inclined. I affix before the door of the hive a piece of wire-work resembling the half of a round mousetrap, and by this very simple means a bee is permitted to return to its house, or take wing as it pleases, without let, stop, or stay from this wicked hypocrite and his companions. This precaution being taken, I endeavour to

THE ENEMIES OF OUR HONEY-BEE.

encourage all mischievous birds to abide with me, feeding the several tom-tits, to each of whom our gardens are so largely indebted, throughout the winter, with walnuts, and even providing them with sleeping places.—Yours, C. S. S."

The woodpecker is another enemy to our hive inhabitants, a serious one too; he does not come into the garden, but follows the bee unceasingly when busy in the fields, and more especially when gathering honey-dew in the early mornings, before the sun has acquired much power. Many of these birds when shot have been found with their stomachs nearly filled with bees. These birds are now becoming so rare that it is scarcely necessary to refer to them.

Let us not overlook this important fact in considering birds as bee-enemies, they principally destroy drones, not the worker bees. This assertion may be hard to prove, yet I think I can make it clear. How do they know the difference between the worker bee and the drones? They may not actually be able at sight to detect the difference, but they are seldom (that is the majority of birds) known to destroy them except in the afternoon, and it is only in the afternoon when drones take wing; again, drones do not fly nearly so fast as the worker bee, and are with more ease caught when on the wing. I do not give this thought to my readers as solely my own, for the same thought is thrown out by two of our best authors of recent times on apiculture.

It must be acknowledged our domestic fowls are exceedingly partial to bees, and I have been inclined to mercilessly condemn them, but I do not now think so hardly about these useful birds, after watching hens, especially at the mouth of the hive, where they have been standing far more unconcerned than even the bee-eating toad, snapping up bee after bee, but they have, I firmly believe, in every instance been only drones. Can we not spare a few thousands of the male bees out of every hive? Let it be remembered they gather no honey and make no wax, yet they consume an enormous quantity of the finest virgin honey. If the birds could not in some degree discriminate betwixt a drone and a worker, how would the queen escape when flying through the air on her wedding flight? She would be gobbled up by some hungry swallow; thus her life would ingloriously terminate, instead of her becoming the mother of thousands and the honoured head of the community. In birds which after being watched busy catching bees on the wing, then shot, upon examination of the stomachs, nothing but drones have been detected. Therefore protect the poor birds; do not yet upon such slender evidence condemn them as bee-murderers.

In America the king bird is doubtless very destructive to the apiaries; he has, however, one redeeming quality, he drives away the crow from the corn-fields. Mr. Hector St. John took as many as 171 dead bees from the craw of one of these birds. They must have been killed only a very short time, as, upon laying them out like corpses upon a blanket in the sun, fifty-four came to life, licked themselves clean, then humming their thanks for delivery from death they joyously went back to their homes. Many tales of this kind are told, such as the recovery of flies found in Madeira wine perhaps two or three years old. An instance is related by Wildman, who states that his informant was a gentleman worthy of credit. He said the Madeira had been brought in bottles from Virginia to London, and that the flies, when exposed to a warm sun for an hour or two, were so completely reanimated as to take wing, thus putting to the test the truth of the opinion that a fly cannot be drowned.

Of this adherence to life, advantage has been taken at the time of deprivation—recourse having been had to immersion for removing a portion of the combs; the bees were afterwards spread on a cloth in the sun and became reanimated. Dr. Derham says that he has known bees revive after remaining twenty-four hours under an exhausted air pump. After long immersion the proboscis of the bee is generally unfolded and stretched to its full length. The first symptom of returning animation is a motion at its extremity, succeeded by a similar motion at the extremities of the legs. Having so far progressed towards recovery, the tongue is soon folded up again, and the bee prepared to resume its customary occupations.

Our friends may take heart, if they should unfortunately find their skeps after a heavy thunderstorm totally immersed in water, and the bees apparently drowned and past recovery. I had a hive, in which a large hole was cut out of the straw at the top, some four inches in diameter, for the purpose of feeding, &c. Partly through sheer forgetfulness I left it exposed; a very heavy storm came on, which continued with very slight intermission for twenty-four hours. I thought surely they must all have perished, for hundreds were washed out of the hive through the mouth, on the ground beneath the stands. What was my joy, when I discovered them the following day, which fortunately turned out fine and warm, buzzing their wings, and humming in real gladness of heart! Those on the floor also recovered under the heat of the sun, and I do not think I lost a single bee. Oil, such as olive or sweet oil, is destructive to bees; if brushed over their sides, just beneath the wings, it causes death like poison in a few minutes, because it stops the breathing, which is performed by pores along the side of the abdomen.

THE WORST BEE-ENEMIES.

Not unfrequently, if the eyes are used carefully in early summer, when rambling in some secluded village lane, or peeping beneath the overhanging eaves of the thatched cottage, we shall discover the nest of the wood-wasp (*Vespa sylvestris*). If it is found in its early stage, or when just completed, and before the architect has had time to deposit eggs in the cells, it may be detached and carried away without fear. I cannot point my readers to a more interesting object than this nest, a paper nest, more like in its external resemblance to a flower made with fine tissue-paper than anything with which I am acquainted: no one can look at it without being filled with admiration at the elegance of its structure and design. They are not so rare as some people imagine: the real fact is, few persons, perhaps, have ever looked carefully for them, or they would doubtless long since have met with one. This species is more common in the north of England than in the southern counties, although they occur here and there all over the land.

Having discovered one of these pretty little nests, and hung it up by means of a little glue to the top of the interior of a glass shade, as a chimney-shelf ornament, we should like to know a little about the history of these wonderful paper-manufacturers. If it be quite correct to describe our honey-bees as the first wax-makers, would it not be equally correct and appropriate to describe these little active, though certainly irascible insects (the wasps), as the first paper-makers? They have known from the days of Adam how to make into paper almost every material which has been used for this purpose in modern times, long before the learned Egyptians employed the leaves of the papyrus, from whence we derive our word paper, to make into books or for writing materials.

First, about the nest and its construction. Carefully turn it over, or glance beneath, and you observe at the base a small orifice (see the engraving); this is the mouth or entrance. At the side, often about the centre, is a rim of paper completely encircling the nest, and cemented to the sides; this is designed very probably to carry off the rain without injuring the inner coat. Sometimes there are two, and I have seen as many as four, rims or hoods; when there are several hoods, it has then, when inverted, a very close resemblance to a double flower. By comparing the outer envelope which surrounds the nest of the common wasp, we shall find it is made of much the same kind of material as that of the wood-wasp. In my

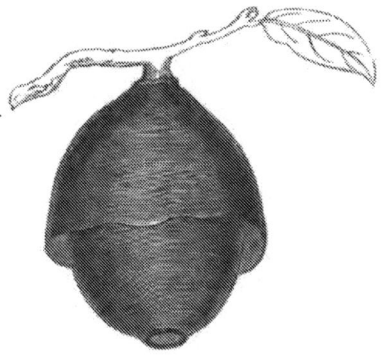

NEST OF THE WOOD-WASP (VESPA SYLVESTRIS).

country rambles, when lounging by the old wooden stile in our village, the two large posts of which are ash boughs, put carelessly or roughly together by our jack-of-all-trades the wheelwright, I have seen at various times scores of wasps busily engaged taking away the wood to form their nests. For two years, the bark not being removed from the wood, they actually made holes in the bark, then from an excavation beneath secured the object of their toil. But with all my watching I have never seen a single wood-wasp working on the ash stile; but I have observed one or two actively employed on an old sycamore tree, and on one occasion I caught one on a bench made from birch-wood. In the *Journal of a Naturalist* it is said they procure their material from the willow and on an allied species, the sallow; I have, however, not been so fortunate as to find them on this wood, although we have plenty of it exposed and decaying about the village. Whatever kind of wood is laboriously scraped together by these insects, it is doubtless some soft white wood, and it is afterwards cemented with what has been named animal glue, but wood alone is not used; withered leaves, fibres of plants, the down from the willow catkin, as well as downy hairs from many leafy buds, are made use of by these active paper-manufacturers.

Wasps abound most in woody, wild districts. I have noticed in one wild woodland in Cheshire that wasps abound in such prodigious quantities that the peasantry have frequently informed me they cannot from this cause keep bees. One cottager in particular had four large colonies of bees in his garden last summer, strong enough, I thought, to resist any foe; however, every stock was destroyed in the autumn by wasps. In another district, about five miles from the above, not woody, but highly cultivated, it is almost a novelty to find a wasp's nest.

There are six distinct species of wasp in the British Islands, seven if we include the hornet, which, after all, is a wasp of a larger size, and all the species manufacture paper for their homes, although some use coarser materials than others, therefore their nests look more rough and uneven; sometimes in a large nest we notice the paper of several shades of colour—this is because it has been put together by many different labourers, using several different kinds of materials. Let us closely watch that sharp little fellow on an old decaying rail; stand perfectly still, and he will fearlessly labour close to your face. It scrapes away bit by bit, seldom moving more than an inch from the place selected, until it has rolled up a good-sized pellet, then grasps it in its strong mandibles (jaws), and flies away to its nest. Having arrived (if it luckily escapes the hungry bird) at its domicile, it retires to rest for a little while—not for long, however, as time seems to be precious. Then we observe it with a pellet of wood, with its legs astride the outer margin, unrolling it carefully; as it unrolls it is firmly flattened or pressed, and glued down: then it rapidly goes over its work again and again, putting a touch here, and adding a little fresh saliva there, until it seems satisfied with its work. This process is repeated day by day until the nest is completed.

The foundation of the nest is laid by a solitary (we might say lonely) queen. After she has laboured several days the structure looks like a tiny umbrella; an appropriate name would be " the fairies' parasol." Let us not forget the fact, when tempted to destroy "the horrid yellow things" of nervous people: she builds the home, lays the eggs, which are fastened securely to the bottom of the cell, and, when these begin to hatch, she has to feed them as well as to carry on the task of building.

Not only are wasps enemies to the honey-bee, but the gardener often finds that, if not watched most carefully, they will make sad havoc among his juicy wall-fruits. However, they do some little good by preying upon the thousands of aphides which sometimes overrun our standard and other roses. This kind of food seems to be a dainty morsel for the young wasps.

Dr. Ormerod mentions instances where the entire destruction of wasps has resulted in swarms of flies, almost as bad as the Egyptian plague in the days of Moses. Wasps certainly do much good as scavengers in destroying a large quantity of decaying vegetable matter; but it is as destroyers of flies, spiders, aphides, caterpillars, and other insects, that their chief good is seen. Examine the ground beneath a large nest, and it is astonishing what a quantity of wings, &c., of flies are seen. In one of my rambles I fortunately witnessed a deadly combat between a ground-wasp and a large spider. For a considerable time it was doubtful which would prove the victor; at length the wasp took a mean advantage over its adversary, and inflicted its sting in the lower part of the spider's body; in a few moments after the spider was dead. I expected, knowing that wasps are carnivorous, to see the victor carry away its spoil, but it appeared to be quite exhausted, and, instead, languidly took wing and disappeared; in about ten minutes it returned with a companion, who severed the body in twain, when it was easily carried away to the nest.

A few years since I witnessed the destruction of a fine apiary solely by wasps, so that in October every stock was destroyed. In some villages wasps are more numerous than in others, but in any case "to be forewarned is to be forearmed." Against this, as against other enemies that may creep inside the hive, such as mice, honey-moth, &c. the best defence is to make the entrance small, and you need not fear a host of them.

During damp weather I noticed underneath one of my bee-stands three small holes somewhat like those made by mice, but scarcely so large. One evening about twilight as several stragglers were making their way towards the hive, evidently quite tired and weary, two of them missed the entrance and dropped to the ground. No sooner did they touch the soil than they were, as quick as thought, conveyed down the holes we had previously observed. Not liking this destruction, and feeling sympathy for the worn-out and tired bees, I procured a shovel, determined to unearth the thief and murderer whatever it was; for the bees had disappeared too rapidly for me to make out the nature of the depredator. Digging down a few inches I found a blackbeetle or cockroach—I am not confident which, as it was injured with the shovel, but I believe it to have been the former insect. However, I have kept a strict watch since, and whenever I have discovered these sly burrows I pour down a few drops of carbolic acid, which not only destroys the inmate but renders the home for a long time tenantless. I was not aware until recently that dragon-flies destroyed bees. Standing in the garden of a friend who owns a large apiary, I saw several large dragon-flies flying about. "Watch that fellow," sharply exclaimed my friend. I did watch, and saw him catch several bees as they were returning to their hive heavily laden, and bear them to a large chestnut tree, where he speedily completed his work and returned to the slaughter again. This was repeated several times, greatly, I confess, to my astonishment. The garden was close to a marshy tract of land. This may, perhaps, account for the appearance of these enemies, as I never noticed them near my own apiary.

SUPERSTITIOUS NOTIONS RESPECTING BEES.

One would have thought that in this nineteenth century these foolish notions respecting our industrious and innocent honey-bees would have become extinct; yet this is not the case in the minds of many ignorant and illiterate country people. All over England, if not in other parts of Great Britain, these superstitions are still in active existence; some few of the most common I will try to place before my readers.

First, it is thought to be very unlucky to purchase bees, and many individuals who really love bees could not be persuaded on any account to give in exchange either silver or gold for them. If this notion generally existed, what would some of our practical apiarians do? They would soon have to relinquish the trade for one more profitable. The plan adopted by these squeamish people is to persuade their neighbours to give them a swarm; then, when they have established an apiary, it is given back in honey in return. I am quite willing to give a hive to any poor cottager who really cannot afford to purchase a swarm; but when I inquire the reason why they wish me to give them the stock, and am told it is because the bees would not prosper if they were purchased, I invariably refuse to give the swarm, for the simple reason that I do not wish to encourage such a foolish idea. Most persons who hold this idea would rather relinquish all the profits attendant upon bee-keeping than purchase a stock, even if it were offered for one shilling.

Again, on the death of any of the bee-keeper's family, the bees must be informed, or the stocks would either die or leave the apiary. One way of doing this is to tap gently on the top of the hive with the key from the front door, and in tones sufficiently loud to be heard inside the hive to tell the active inmates the name of the person, and the day of his or her death. Another plan is to place black crape round the hive for a certain period. Passing by the garden of a poor widow some time since, I ventured to examine the hives, which I usually do if time will permit, and sometimes in addition tender a little advice, to those willing to listen, upon their profitable management. I was rather surprised to find all the hives tenantless; upon inquiring the reason why they were all dead, I was informed it was because they had omitted to remind them of her husband's decease. "They did not die," she strenuously maintained, "but all forsook their hives and went away." I had the greatest difficulty to persuade her they had actually died during the previous winter or spring from starvation. She scarcely credited what I said even when I turned up the hives one by one and exhibited the dead bees by thousands; and, after all, when leaving her garden, she declared I was for once mistaken, for the bees must have gone away to some more hospitable place.

In Switzerland, upon the death of any of the household, the hives even in the depth of winter are turned upside-down when the funeral procession is leaving the house for the churchyard. A rather amusing instance of this superstition is narrated by Langstroth. The coffin containing the deceased was left exposed for a time outside the house, not far from the bees'-stand, on a hot summer's day, when several bees alighted upon the coffin and commenced a happy, cheerful humming sound (invariably emitted when pleased). The relatives believed they were mourning the death of their master. On the contrary, they were delighted to find such a quantity of good propolis oozing from the pine-wood, and perhaps their hive just at the time stood in great need of this article.

When conveying bees from one part of the country to another they must not be carried over running water, or they will assuredly die, or prove unproductive and unprofitable. It sometimes is difficult to avoid, if carrying them any distance, coming across a brook or other running stream; yet I have known them carried three or four miles in a circular direction rather than go over any rivulet.

I seldom hear this notion expressed now; it is several years since I heard it from an aged peasant.

In some parts of the north of England the 10th of August is considered as a day of jubilee amongst bees. Why, I cannot tell. A swarm coming out on this day would not be hived under any circumstances, because they are said to be unlucky. Bees working on this day are named Quakers, perhaps because the members of the Society of Friends observe no holiday. This is near akin to the idea that the bees should not be allowed to quit the hive on Friday; many apiarians belonging to the Roman Catholic persuasion, I am informed, carry this out literally by closing the entrance or the mouth of the hive on that day.

A swarm of bees settling upon a dead tree, or a hedge-stake, or rail, which is considered "dead wood," is a sign or token of death, *i.e.*, it predicts the death of some member of the family to whom they belong. A poor fellow with whom I was sympathising upon the death of his wife said to me, "I expected some one of us would be laid in the grave-yard before long." "Why?" said I, in reply. "Because," he answered, "the swarm of bees which came out first this season settled on the hedge-rail. When they settle on dead or dying wood it is always a token of death, and I have never known it to fail." It is accounted unlucky for a swarm of bees to settle on your premises unless they are claimed by their owner and given up to him peaceably. Several years since a strong stock settled in an apple-tree in the garden of one of my neighbours. It would not have been very difficult, perhaps, to name the actual owner of this stray swarm, but the old gentleman in whose apple-tree they were clustered was by no means willing to part with them. Some of the neighbours whispered, "Ah! you'll see the old man, or his older wife, will die before long." Accordingly it came to

SUPERSTITIONS RESPECTING BEES. 173

pass; the kind master of the house was shortly afterwards carried to his long home. This appeared to confirm the prediction, and the whispering neighbours and village gossips now point to this as an instance of the truth of the old saying.

I was lately looking over the stocks in what was once a fine and flourishing apiary, but it appeared to have suffered severe losses. I was perplexed to account for the death of so many stocks, except by starvation, which is the case in by far the majority of instances, but I was not left long in doubt, if the word of one of the domestic servants was to be credited. "Why, master," she exclaimed, before I left the premises, "you need not be astonished, for I have heard it said scores of times that bees will never thrive if folks fight about them." "Well, but you don't mean to say that any one fights about your bees," I replied. "If they don't fight with their fists," she answered rather pettishly, "they fight with words, and that is every bit as bad. And I say again, and go where you will you'll find my words true, bees will never do any good for anybody if they fight about them, for they are peaceable things, and knowing things too, those bees are, and they know well enough when anybody is vexed with them."

A great horror exists in the minds of not a few intelligent rustic bee-keepers against what they are pleased to term the new-fangled notion of driving the stocks into empty skeps in the autumn when taking the honey, and afterwards mingling them with other stocks well provided with food, instead of cruelly destroying them over the brimstone pit. I believe they have an idea that something unlucky will befal themselves or their families should the stocks be driven and preserved.

A NORTH AMERICAN BEE-HUNT.

BY WASHINGTON IRVING.

The beautiful forest in which we were encamped abounded in bee-trees; that is to say, trees in the decayed trunks of which wild bees had established their hives. It is surprising in what countless swarms the bees have overspread the Far West within but a moderate number of years. The Indians consider them the harbinger of the white man, as the buffalo is of the red man; and say, that in proportion as the bee advances the Indian and the buffalo retire. We are always accustomed to associate the hum of the bee-hive with the farm-house and the flower-garden, and to consider those industrious little insects as connected with the busy haunts of men; and I am told that the wild bee is seldom to be met with at any distance from the frontier. They have been the heralds of civilization, steadily preceding it as it advanced from the Atlantic borders; and some of the ancient settlers of the Far West pretend to give the very year when the honey-bee first crossed the Mississippi. The Indians with surprise found the mouldering trees of their forests suddenly teeming with ambrosial sweets; and nothing, I am told, can exceed the greedy relish with which they banquet for the first time upon this unbought luxury of the wilderness.

At present the honey-bee swarms in myriads in the noble groves and forests that skirt and intersect the prairies, and extend along the alluvial bottoms of the rivers. It seems to me as if these beautiful regions answer literally to the description of the land of promise, "a land flowing with milk and honey;" for the rich pasturage of the prairies is calculated to sustain herds of cattle as countless as the sands upon the seashore, while the flowers with which they are enamelled render them a very paradise for the nectar-seeking bee.

We had not been long in the camp when a party set out in quest of a bee-tree; and, being curious to witness the sport, I gladly accepted an invitation to accompany them. The party was headed by a veteran bee-hunter, a tall, lank fellow, in homespun garb, that hung loosely about his limbs, and a straw hat shaped not unlike a bee-hive; a comrade equally uncouth in garb, and without a hat, straddled along at his heels, with a long rifle on his shoulder. To these succeeded half a dozen others, some with axes and some with rifles; for no one stirs far from camp without fire-arms, so as to be ready either for wild deer or savage Indian.

After proceeding some distance we came to an open glade on the skirts of the forest. Here our leader halted, and then advanced quietly to a low bush, on the top of which I perceived a piece of honeycomb. This I found was the bait or lure for the wild bees. Several were humming about it, and diving into its cells. When they had laden themselves with honey they would rise up in the air, and dart off in one straight line, almost with the velocity of a bullet. The hunters watched attentively the course they took, and then set off in the same direction, stumbling along over twisted roots and fallen trees, with their eyes turned up to the sky. In this way they traced the honey-laden bees to their hive, in the hollow trunk of a blasted oak, where, after buzzing about for a moment, they entered a hole about sixty feet from the ground,

Two of the bee-hunters now applied their axes vigorously at the foot of the tree to level it with the ground. The mere spectators and amateurs, in the meantime, drew off to a cautious distance, to be out of the way of the falling of the tree and the vengeance of its inmates. The jarring blows of the axe seemed to have no effect in alarming or agitating this most industrious community. They continued to ply at their usual occupations, some arriving full freighted into port, others sallying forth on new expeditions, like so many merchantmen in a money-making metropolis, little suspicious of impending bankruptcy and downfall. Even a loud crack which announced the disrupture of the trunk failed to divert their attention from the intense pursuit of gain; at length down came the tree with a tremendous crash, bursting open from end to end, and displaying all the hoarded treasures of the commonwealth.

One of the hunters immediately ran up with a wisp of lighted hay as a defence against the bees. The latter, however, made no attack and sought no revenge; they seemed stupefied by the catastrophe, and unsuspicious of its cause, and remained crawling and buzzing about the ruins, without offering us any molestation. Every one of the party now fell to, with spoon and hunting knife, to scoop out the flakes of honeycomb with which the hollow trunk was stored. Some of them were of very old date, and of a deep brown colour; others were beautifully white, and the honey in their cells was almost limpid. Such of the combs as were entire were placed in camp kettles, to be conveyed to the encampment, those which had been shivered by the fall were devoured upon the spot. Every stark bee-hunter was to be seen with a morsel in his hand, dripping about his fingers, and disappearing as rapidly as a cream-tart before the holiday appetite of a school-boy.

Nor was it the bee-hunters alone who profited by the downfall of this industrious community. As if the bees would carry through the similitude of their habits with those of laborious and gainful man, I beheld numbers from rival hives arriving on eager wings to enrich themselves with the ruin of their neighbours. These busied themselves as eagerly and cheerily as so many wreckers on an Indiaman which has been driven on shore—plunging into the cells of the broken combs, banqueting greedily on the spoil, and then winging their way full-freighted to their homes. As to the poor proprietors of the ruin, they seemed to have no heart to do anything, not even to taste the nectar that flowed around them, but crawled backwards and forwards in vacant desolation, as I have seen a poor fellow, with his hands in his breeches pockets, whistling vacantly and despondingly about the ruins of his house which had been burnt.

It is difficult to describe the bewilderment and confusion of the bees of the bankrupt hive, who had been absent at the time of the catastrophe, and who arrived from time to time with full cargoes from abroad. At first they wheeled about the air, in the place where the fallen tree had once reared its head, astonished at finding all a vacuum. At length, as if comprehending their disaster, they settled down in clusters on a dry branch of a neighbouring tree, from whence they seemed to contemplate the prostrate ruin, and to buzz forth doleful lamentations over the downfall of their republic. It was a scene in which the "melancholy Jacques" might have moralised by the hour. We now abandoned the place, leaving much honey in the hollow of the tree. "It will be all cleared off by varmint," said one of the rangers. "What vermin?" said I. "Oh! bears and skunks, and possums, and racoons. The bears is the knowing'st varmint for finding out a bee-tree in the world. They'll gnaw for days together at the trunk, till they make a hole big enough to get in their paws, and then they'll hole out honey, bees, and all."

AUSTRALIAN BEE-HUNTING.

From the absence of flowers in many parts of the bush of Australia, the little native bee may be seen busily working on the bark of the trees, and, unlike the bees of this country, which are ever on the move from flower to flower, it seems to be unconscious of danger. This may arise from the vastness of the solitudes in Australia, which are seldom if ever disturbed, except by a passing tribe, or by its own wild denizens, which are far from numerous. The bee is therefore easily approached, and the bright clear atmosphere of the climate is peculiarly favourable to the pursuit. A party of two or three natives, armed with a tomahawk, sally forth into the bush, having previously provided themselves with the soft white down from the breast of some bird, which is very light in texture and at the same time very fluffy.

With that wonderful quickness of sight which practice has rendered perfect, they descry the little brownish leaden-coloured insect on the bark, and, rolling up an end of the down feather to the finest possible point between the fingers, they dip it into a gummy substance which a peculiar sort of herb exudes when the stem is broken. They then cautiously approach the bee, and with great delicacy of touch place the gummed point under the hind legs of the bee. It at once adheres. Then comes the result for which all this preparation has been made. The bee feeling the additional weight fancies he has done his task and is laden with honey, and flies off the tree on his homeward journey at no great distance from the ground. The small white feather is now all that can be discerned, and the hunt at once commences. Running on foot amid broken branches and stony ground requires, one would think, the aid of one's eyesight; but with the native Australians it is not so. Without taking for a moment their eyes off the object, they follow it, sometimes to the distance of half-a-mile, and rarely, if ever, fail in marking the very branch where they saw the little bit of white down disappear at the entrance of the hive. Here there is a halt, the prize is found, and they sit down to regain their breath before ascending the tree, and to light a pipe—to which old and young, men, women, and children, are extremely partial. When the rest and smoke are over, with one arm round the tree and the tomahawk in the other, the black man cuts notches in the bark, and, placing the big toe in the notches, ascends this hastily constructed stair until he comes to where the branches commence; then, putting the handle of the tomahawk between his teeth, he climbs with the ease and agility of a monkey till he reaches the branch where last he saw the white down disappear; he then carefully sounds the branches with the back of his tomahawk till the dull and distinct sound from the hollow tells him where the hive is.

A hole is then cut, and he puts his hand in and takes the honey out. If alone, the savage eats when up the tree till he can eat no more and leaves the rest; but, if with others, he cuts a square piece of bark, and, after having had the best part of the hive as a reward for his exertions, brings down a mass of honey and comb mixed together, which, though not inviting, is greedily devoured by those below.

In one of Cooper's novels, I think the "Oak Openings," will be found a wonderful description of a bee-hunt, similar in its mode to the above.

THE BEE-HUNTER.

Whether the honey-bee (*Apis mellifica*) is a native of the New World, or whether it was carried there by some of the Pilgrim Fathers, is not known, though it has been observed by the Indians to be never far distant from the borders of civilisation. Long ago the invasion of Kentucky by Boone and the other pioneer backwoodsmen is said to have been foretold by a Shawnee warrior, who, seeing a bee on the western bank of the Mississippi, warned his tribe that before very long their hunting-grounds would be invaded; and, later still, the settlement of California was predicted by a Gumas Indian, on discovering a bee-tree on the Gila river. In some of the south-western states, the collection of wild honey, as an article of barter or trade, has been made a business by some of the backwoodsmen; and as honey used to bring a quarter of a dollar a gallon, and some of the bee-trees yielded from six to a dozen gallons of honey, besides wax, it was not an unprofitable pursuit. The taste that leads a man to take delight in the boisterous music of a pack of deer-hounds, as they drive the stag to a stand, or in the rough danger of a bear-fight, is not a proper foundation upon which to build the bee-hunter. The bee-hunter is of a pensive turn, fond of solitude, fond of nature, delighting in flowers, though perhaps not from a botanical point of view. If he reads, he has probably read Burton's "Anatomy of Melancholy;" most certainly he has read and re-read, time after time, Izaak Walton's "Complete Angler," for there is no such anomaly as a bee-hunter who is not also a patient, skilful piscator. So fond is he of the silence of the woods, whose stillness is only broken by the drowsy hum of a bee, or the gentle chirp of a bird, that the occasional sharp tap tap of the woodpecker sounds harshly to his ear.

On the bank of some navigable stream the bee-hunter builds his log-cabin, fences in an acre or two of ground to grow his vegetables upon, depends for meat upon his trusty rifle, and for his bread upon his skill in detecting the stores of the wild bees; and, when he has collected three or four barrels of honey, he rolls them down the bluff river-bank and into his boat, and paddling his cargo off to the nearest settlement, returns with a barrel of flour, powder, lead, or any necessaries he may be in need of. If he has settled upon one of the larger streams where the great river steam-boats ply, such as the Mississippi, he generally trades with the captain of some boat, thereby saving his time, yet perhaps at a slight sacrifice, as the captain will expect to make a little by the trade, though the freight on his own boat will be nothing, and the better price the honey will command at New Orleans will leave the skipper a fair margin for profit.

The "Father of Waters," as the Mississippi has been poetically named, is a very bad translation of its true meaning. The name is derived from the once most powerful tribe of the South-west, the Choctaws, and in their language the two adjectives, *Missah* and *Sippah*, when separate, are used constantly to qualify the most familiar things; but when compounded they serve to give the characteristic name to this immense river—*Missah*, old, big; *sippah*, strong—Old-Big-Strong.

The difference between a bee-hunter and an ordinary man strikes the observer at once. Relying upon the qualities of his mind, he has a profound contempt for the mere adornment of his person. An old battered sombrero, whose broad brim shades his eyes, graces his head; a blue and white striped hickory shirt, unfastened at the throat, and indeed not buttoned anywhere, hangs negligently on his shoulders; coat or waistcoat is dispensed with altogether, whilst his "unmentionables" are of deer-skin, stained about equally with dirt and honey, and, if of less durable materials, are fringed with numberless ribbons, giving evidence of many a briar and brake that he has plunged heedlessly through when his eye has been intent on "lining" some bee to its nest.

Then the perfection to which he has educated his eye is wonderful; for to his powers of vision he is principally indebted for his success.

By the law of the woods, whoever finds a bee-tree and marks it by cutting a strip or two of bark off is entitled to it at any future time; and any one who should be mean enough to fell and take the honey from that blazed tree would be looked upon as a thief quite as much as though he had picked his neighbour's pocket; and, to the honour of the thousands of backwoodsmen I have known, I have never heard of a single instance where this rule has not been respected.

"How many bee-trees have you marked this summer?" said I to an old negro, who was busily mending a broken axe-handle.

"Ninety-four, massa, and come fall I 'spects to have a power of honey to trade."

These trees had all been marked in the neighbourhood of the plantation; and, though probably the negro himself would never be able to find all the trees again, yet being marked they would not be interfered with though a dozen honey-hunters passed them.

In my forest wanderings I have repeatedly come upon a bee-tree, only marking it when it was near some settlement, as I never had any intention of cutting down one of the largest trees of the forest, only to be rewarded for my trouble by getting thoroughly well stung. In Africa the honey-bird *(Indicator Vaillantii)* is a sure guide to the Hottentots. Directed by its shrill cry the hunter follows the bird, endeavouring always to keep it in sight, and tracks its course wherever it may lead. In America we have no corresponding guide, and either find the honey by accident, or by hunting for it as I am now about to describe.

It was a beautiful autumnal morning that I set out to meet Tony Sneed, the bee-hunter, by appointment, on a prairie near the edge of the San Bernard River. Tony was true to time, a curved-handled Collins axe in his hand, and a tin bucket on his shoulder, followed by his son, a great gawky lad of seventeen or eighteen, who also bore an axe and a couple of buckets. We had scarcely exchanged salutations when Tony, throwing out his arm —the one thrust through the pail handle—exclaimed,

"Thar goes a bee right for that point of timber. He was a loaded bee," he added meditatively, "for his thighs were as yellow as a California gold miner's legs. I can see a bee for a very long distance on a clear day; howsumever we've got one lined."

His preparations were beautiful from their simplicity. An old tin copper-cap box about half filled with honey, a common blue saucer, a glass tumbler, and a little phial of flour of sulphur, constituted Tony's stock in trade.

Blue, yellow, red, and white autumn flowers carpeted the prairie, and amongst them several bees were flitting; occasionally four or five would be upon one weed, and when Tony's glance fell upon them he would observe, "Them's almost allus from one tree; what I wants is scattered bees to line and angle from." I fancied I knew what he meant by line, but angle from was beyond my comprehension, and I asked him, "How do you mean angle from?"

"Ef you'll have a little patience, you'll see all's one as well as my telling."

Thus rebuked for my curiosity, I could only watch Tony's proceedings in silence.

Reversing the tin bucket, he set it upon the ground, and upon it placed the saucer, into which he poured about half a teaspoonful of honey, and drawing off a yard or so patiently waited.

The smell of the honey soon attracted one bee, then another, and presently five bees were busy upon the honey in the saucer. Cautiously approaching the saucer an inch at a time, Tony, by a sudden and dexterous movement, placed the tumbler over the bees, and over this again his hat, remarking, as he did so, "They works harder in the dark." In about three minutes Tony raised his weather-beaten hat, and minutely inspected the first bee which had settled upon the saucer, and after this examination he pronounced the insect "about filled." Taking a pinch of the sulphur flour between the finger and thumb of his right hand, and raising the saucer in his left, he stood watching for the bee to fly, and the moment it did so, and had cleared the edge of the saucer, it was lightly dusted with the sulphur. "There'll be a muss in the hive when that chap gets home," said Tony; "it's gone right for the same place as the first one I noticed afore I set the sarcer." In a few minutes another flew, and was sulphur-dusted as was the first, and this too, Tony said, went in the same direction as the other. A third was served in the same way; but this, unlike the others, flew towards another point of the timber, which satisfied Tony that it belonged to a different tree. The bee-hunter spoke confidently of seeing the bees, long after they were out of my sight; and although my eyes had served a long apprenticeship in the pursuit of game, both in the forest and on the prairie, yet, strain them as I would, I lost sight of the bees at less than two hundred yards' distance, so that I could only conclude that by very long and ceaseless practice Sneed had acquired his keenness of vision. Moving about two hundred yards to the right of our first position, the bee-hunter again prepared his honey saucer, secured some bees, and repeated his experiment. This was to get the angle; and this, as it was explained to me, was done in this manner:—It seems that the organ of locality is so strongly developed in the bee that when it has loaded itself with honey it starts off immediately in a straight line for home; and so well is this characteristic known by the American hunters, that it is a common saying with them, when starting in a hurry, to say, "Well, I shall make a bee-line for home," or for any other place which they wish to reach at once. A bee-hunter then, having found the line of his bee, has only half performed his task; for the home of the bee may be a mile or two deep in the forest; but by taking a different position and a fresh bee, and marking where the point of intersection would be of the two flights, he can judge pretty well how deep in the forest the hive will be, as the two bees, if belonging to the same tree, will converge from their opposite starting points to the tiny hole by which they enter their home in the arm of some great forest tree. Practice enables the hunter to determine this in half the time it takes to explain it, even as lamely as I have done, and gathering up his various implements he starts in pursuit. Arrived in the neighbourhood of the tree, the reason why the sulphur was used is apparent; the dusted bees had disturbed all the other inmates of their little community by the disagreeable taint they had brought with them; and now the buzzing, humming noise of the colony directs Tony to his prey.

The tree at whose foot we had arrived was one of the finest in the forest. For two centuries at least it had stretched its giant limbs towards the heavens, and its green leaves had fluttered in the summer breeze long before its destroyer's grandfather was born; "but the axe was laid to the root of the tree," and, whilst Tony Sneed plied his strokes thick and fast on one side, his son's blows sounded quick and sharp on the other. Until the tree began to totter, the bees had not seemed aware that any danger threatened their home, but as soon as they understood the nature of the invasion they sallied out to attack the invaders; and, though they inflicted many a sting, Sneed and his son were equal to the occasion. Ceasing from their chopping, they collected some brush and moss, and, piling them up into two or three heaps, set them on fire, and soon the rank smoke made the bees beat a hasty retreat, whilst Tony and his son, resuming their labours, soon brought the forest giant to the ground. For myself I had kept at a respectful distance when the bees began to attack, though near enough to watch all the proceedings. As soon as the tree was down Sneed and his son built "a smoke," at about four or five feet distance all around the limb which contained the honey; and, this effected, the philosopher, lighting his pipe, joined me. "I don't like to kill the critters," he remarked, "though I want their honey. The smoke 'll drive them off, and they'll soon find another hollow. Them as it don't drive off it will only suffocate for a while, and they'll come to as fresh as paint an hour after we are gone."

When the bees had been thoroughly driven off, we took some small biscuits, called crackers, from our pockets, and, dipping them in virgin honey, made our lunch, after which Sneed and his son filled their buckets, and we started homewards, having witnessed for the first time a scientific bee-hunt.

How thoroughly the senses of the back-woodsman are cultivated the following quotation from a friend will show: "The forest hunter is compelled to cultivate his sight to almost the same degree of perfection that characterises the touch of the blind, and experience at last renders it so keen that the slightest touch of a passing object on the leaves, trees, or earth, leaves to him a deep and visible impression, though to the common eye unseen as the path of the bird through the air. This knowledge governs the chase and the war-path; this knowledge is what, when excelled in, makes the master spirit among the rude inhabitants of the wood: and that man is the greatest chief who follows the coldest trail, and leaves none behind him by his own footsteps."

GOLDEN RULES FOR BEE-FARMERS.

We extract the following notes from a kind of bee-diary—or rather notes of an amateur's work in apiarian matters, trusting they may be useful to those who are inexperienced in these things, and thus prevent loss, and, what is even worse to some people, disappointment. Many of our friends who have commenced an apiary have given up the pursuit solely because they did not find it all straightforward, and met at first with a few disappointments.

The golden rule in bee-keeping is, "Keep your stocks strong." For the first few years of our bee-keeping we tried to increase our stocks as rapidly as possible. To do this we hived every swarm as a separate colony, and in some seasons our old stocks have thrown off a swarm and two casts. These were all hived in separate skeps, thus making three stocks, where, if we had been wise, there would only have been one. It was what in other things would have been called "making haste to be rich." However, the result was nothing but loss and disappointment the ensuing season.

Some of the casts, or what are generally known as swarms, would not, if measured, have contained a pint of bees. Being so small at the commencement, we could not expect them to make good strong colonies. Perhaps had we been sufficiently wide-awake we could in the autumn have placed in each hive two or three condemned cottagers' stocks, then they might have wintered well, and very likely had a fair start in spring. We fed them liberally with syrup and honey, still they seemed to dwindle gradually away, and the coming spring saw them all dead, or so very feeble and weak as to be worthless.

The reason why we hear such an outcry against bees

and bee-keeping amongst our cottagers is, that this golden rule seems to be completely overlooked. Profitable bee-keeping is a subject much talked about as well as written upon, but somehow or other—perhaps from the fact that people have been so misled by popular publications—the idea has now taken hold of the bee-keepers of this country that there is no such thing as profitable bee-keeping. This is erroneous, and the sooner it is set right the better for everybody. Bee-keeping is without doubt very profitable if you follow the rule—*Keep your stocks strong*. During the past year we were induced, by advertisements seen in one of our monthly periodicals, to purchase two small pamphlets upon apiculture: one was entitled *Keep Bees, Keep Bees*, the French bishop's advice to his poor clergy; *The A.B.C. Guide, or Cottager's Manual*, showing how by proper management ten or twelve stock-hives will return the owner an annual profit of 50*l*. This consisted principally of extracts from other publications. I should, however, like to know whether any one has made 50*l*. in any one year from the old sulphuring system. The other pamphlet was entitled 70*l. a Year; or How I make it by my Bees*. This book informed the reader how to work his apiary; it was upon the nadir system, or we must purchase a lot of American cheese-boxes, and, when the hives show symptoms of swarming, place the cheese-boxes beneath them, feed liberally with sugar, and at the end of the season we should have a golden honey-harvest. I don't think our aristocracy, who like to see a little pure honey in the comb on their breakfast-table, will thank us for syrup cased up in wax. However, I merely mention these books, which have no doubt misled many persons, to warn my readers against following such popular guides: they will only end in disappointment.

I trust my readers will pardon this digression. Now to my subject—Keep your stocks strong. First, I give a little of my experience to prove the correctness of the golden rule. I had four stocks of bees which I worked to prove the rule; three contained perhaps 15,000 bees in each hive; the other or fourth stock was very strong, and perhaps would contain 40,000, if correctly counted. The result in the autumn confirmed my rule; the strong colony stored a third more honey than all the other three stocks; all the summer they worked most industriously, while the weak stocks appeared careless, or to have no heart for labour.

It is a very easy matter to keep your stocks alive and prosperous when the sun shines, or during the summer months, but it is quite different in the winter; then your stocks die away sometimes, and you are scarcely able to tell why. One thing should not be overlooked: If your stocks are strong in the autumn, and have sufficient food to supply them during the whole winter, with a strong vigorous queen at their head, you will have little cause to fear; they will winter well, and come out next spring prepared for another season's labours.

Write out the following and affix it in your apiary, at all events do not let it escape your memory:—"A strong colony will consume much less food during winter than a weak one." This may seem paradoxical, but it is the experience of all the bee-keepers with whom we have conversed, especially of those who are thoroughly acquainted with the habits and economy of the insects. A weak stock is continually moving about in the hive, and do what they will they cannot keep up the temperature except by consuming a large quantity of honey; on the other hand, strong colonies cluster closer together in large masses, and seldom move about; they can thus keep up an even temperature without eating so much food. On this plea it is wiser to keep strong stocks of bees than feeble ones.

All apiarians rejoice when they can secure early swarms. The old saw says:—

> A swarm of bees in May
> Is worth a load of hay.

You may reasonably hope for early swarms only when you keep strong stocks, not otherwise. We trust we have now said sufficient, not alone to convince the practical apiarian, but to induce all our readers who scan the above remarks to keep strong stocks, for then they may expect the apiary to be profitable as well as instructive.

BEE FARMER'S CALENDAR.

WORK FOR JANUARY.

No real work is needful during this the first month of the year; but there are one or two points worthy of attention, and, if we love our bees, nothing will be thought too much trouble. We fear there are many so-called beekeepers who are very careless, and by carelessness alone they allow many of their stocks to die during this and the following two or three months.

Ventilation. Owing to this being overlooked, in the majority of cases, many colonies become diseased and perish. A free current of air should be allowed to run through the entire hive; a good plan is to elevate the top-board about one-eighth of an inch; by this means the air in the hive is kept dry; but when a wooden hive is tightly closed it becomes saturated with moisture; we once lost a most valuable stock from this cause. If the bees which venture on the alighting board at the entrance void a yellow substance, it is a sign they have dysentery; no time must be lost in looking after the stock, if they are to be saved from utter loss.

Mice are very fond of the shelter afforded by straw

hives; they creep in unawares, and, finding a warm comfortable home, with a rich pantry, they are very loth to leave such a pleasant domicile; but oust them out without the least compunction, as they work sad havoc amongst the combs. Birds are on the look-out for solitary bees flying abroad during sunny days; however, we do not think they do much damage, the few bees they gobble up will not be so very great a loss. The only bee-enemy which we dislike is the little tomtit; in straw hives he does a great deal of mischief. In bar-frame hives, neither mice nor birds ever give much trouble.

Take care the entrance is made small, then you need pay no more attention, except it be to shade the entrance if snow be on the ground.

Never entirely close up the mouth of the hive, as we have known many thoughtless bee-keepers do in hard weather. Bees require fresh air as much as we do. It is not cold that kills them, damp is more to be dreaded.

Look up any old hives, repaint them on the outside, and clean them in every nook and corner. If you purpose increasing your stocks during the coming summer, prepare your hives in time; do not leave them to be sought when the swarms are flying abroad. We have invariably found it better to purchase them than to make them ourselves, when they can be bought at all reasonably.

Work for February.

Winter being almost gone, we are apt to imagine the stocks still left alive require no more care or attention. A greater fallacy cannot well be conceived. Now our work must begin in right good earnest.

Lose no time in overhauling your stocks. Having blown a little smoke amongst them, lift the hive bodily from the bottom board, if they are in skeps, and brush off all the dead bees; in fact, carefully clean it from all dirt, &c. which might hinder or impede them in their work.

They are just now enlivened with every gleam of sunshine, and anxious to be abroad, therefore remove every obstacle.

This month, above all others, is rife with disease. By removing the bottom board *dysentery*, &c. is easily detected and by timely warning the stock may be saved. If the hive appears at all damp, lift it up above the bottom board, supporting it about a quarter of an inch all round by thin wedges from about 10 a.m. to 3 p.m. By no means leave the stock thus exposed to night-air; if any snow should fall, especially now, after the bees have commenced their spring flight, close up the entrance for a few hours until the glare has passed away.

Remember more stocks die from sheer want of food after March has come in than at any other period; therefore begin to feed every stock in the apiary very cautiously. This will have a twofold advantage; by feeding them during any warm or dry day the queen will commence depositing brood, thus your stocks will probably throw off very early swarms. We have tested this; we fed three small stocks, commencing the last week in February, and gave each stock about two pounds and a-half of syrup each fortnight, until the second week in April; these stocks threw off each three fine swarms the following summer; but two other hives left unfed only swarmed once, the second week in July; thus feeding proved very profitable.

Another wise thing is to place a shallow dish a little distance from the bee-shed filled with barley-flour. We find our bees will take up a considerable quantity to the hives during mild sunny days; this will be another strong inducement for the queen to begin laying her eggs, for it is doubtless used instead of pollen to feed the young brood.

Very much depends upon early breeding, the stocks soon become strong, throwing off fine swarms, and are in readiness to avail themselves of the honey harvest when it comes.

Work for March.

Bearing in mind the grand rule, "*Keep your stocks strong,*" early in this month, examine each hive carefully, for we can only expect those hives which contain a strong and healthy stock to be profitable.

Look well to the entrance of the hive; if the bees are observed to void a yellowish excrement you have cause to suspect dysentery. This disease is brought on either from dampness or improper and sour food. We have always found the remedy is cleanliness and feeding with good new honey.

If the apiary is composed of straw skeps, *give to each stock* a clean floor board; if this is impossible the sooner the old boards are cleansed the better. In bar-frame hives gently lift up the upper part on a fine warm day and brush all the dead bees, with other dirt, from the bottom board. Bees attend closely to all sanitary matters; in the working season, their dead are speedily carried forth; but in the winter this cannot be done owing to their close confinement; therefore, it is well to aid them in this matter; they will afterwards appreciate and repay the kind forethought.

If they have not commenced soon after the month of March has set in to carry pollen to the hives when the weather is favourable, something is wrong, and the sooner the stock is examined the better. Perhaps they are a queenless colony; if so, unite them to some other stock; the hive with its valuable comb will be reserved for a swarm. If the greater part of the month is cold and frosty, with occasional slight snow-storms, and with scarcely a crocus visible until the third week, we cannot expect to see any pollen carried in. It will then be found useful to continue to place barley-meal within reach; the bees will use it instead of pollen.

If any stock is deficient in food, which may be ascertained by feeling the weight of the hive, give them a small quantity of newly-made syrup each warm afternoon; this will stimulate, and do the colony good; breeding will also go on at a greater rate; but care should be exercised not to smear any syrup or honey on the hive or floor-board, it will entice robbers, and most likely produce fighting. We have used most successfully the best barley-sugar; as this is not stored in the cells, it is easy to ascertain when food is scarce.

The winter aconite (*Eranthis hyemalis*) and various species of spring crocus yield the chief supply of pollen during this month. *Close the entrance* if snow lies on the ground. Hundreds of bees perish from being enticed out by the glare of the sun and snow combined.

Work for April.

Do not forget to encourage your weak stocks by rather liberal feeding every warm evening. You will soon learn when they have sufficient food, for when honey can be gathered your sugar will be left untouched. By neglecting to feed in this month I have, when I began bee-keeping, lost many large stocks. They appeared to be very healthy and lively up to April, when all at once they died of actual starvation. Nothing causes the kind bee-keeper so much sadness in his bee pursuits as this, because the thought will constantly arise in his mind, " I might have saved the poor things if I had not been careless."

Recollect, this is the most dangerous month in the year. Be as active as your bees. A little attention and care bestowed upon them now will be amply repaid by your industrious subjects.

Floor, or bottom boards, if not already attended to, should at once be scrupulously cleansed; if it is not attended to now, on some nice sunny afternoon, it is probable you will never do it. Cut away all the little bits of comb which the bees last season fastened to the floorboard; they are only in the way, and will cause the inmates much annoyance and inconvenience in the busy season now rapidly approaching. I give all the straw skeps in my apiary either a new board, or, at all events, one which was well washed in the summer and laid by until the next spring to sweeten, so that it is equal to a new one. If you have no new ones at hand be sure you scrape the old ones with an old knife, and make them as clean as your own dinner-table. Do not for one moment think it useless to do so, a waste of time, labour, &c. *Try the difference*—clean one hive-board well, and leave the other uncared for—then another year you will remember our advice.

Water.— Observe your bees flying and humming lazily about the water-butts, pump-trough, and the little pools of water about your premises; when they alight watch them eagerly drinking, then flying off to their homes with joy. Bees are all water-drinkers, so every teetotaller should be a bee-keeper. Perhaps in April and May water is more needed than in any other month during the whole year. A friend has a square tin vessel, about three inches deep, placed opposite the stands, in which, when nearly filled with water, he places a quantity of moss; the bees seem to appreciate this contrivance, for they have no fear of death by drowning when running over the moss fronds. I have seen thousands of my neighbours' bees drowned in a water or rain tub reared against his house. The water being low in the tub the bees have been unable to make their escape. Such vessels are veritable death-traps. My bees seldom leave the garden if water is placed conveniently for them. It is surprising how soon they learn where to go for the supply of water for their young brood and cell-building.

Another matter should be attended to this month, although it does not exactly come within the bee-master's scope, yet if he studies the welfare of his stocks he will keep a sharp look out for *Queen Wasps*, which now begin to put in an appearance. Remember each queen wasp commences and sustains a new colony; so every queen destroyed in April in reality destroys a whole nest, or what would be a nest later in the season. It is not uncommon for one queen to rear a nest of fifty thousand. These thieves can soon eat your best honey, not to mention the immense number of working bees which they murder in the fields. Let war to the bitter end be at once and for ever declared against wasps.

Look out for Robbers and Thieves. -- We dread the light-fingered gentry about our houses and homes, but hive-robbers are far worse to deal with. We have just mentioned a thief who is dressed in yellow livery, but the foes which bees evidently dread most are bees from a neighbouring hive, often on the same stand, where several hives are placed close together. Every warm afternoon, if you can spare a few minutes, walk gently round your stocks, and note the entrance of each hive; you will easily detect friend from foe. The thief is buzzing about; when it alights at the mouth of the hive it first peeps in to see if the coast is clear, then, with a quickness not observed in the inmates, he darts into the hive, but often, and always if the stock is strong, as quickly darts out again, pursued by several bees. If robbing is actively going on, the sooner the hive is removed to a new stand the better. Sometimes it is well to remove the hive to a new locality, unknown to the robbers; it is only by this means that the stock can be saved. If it has only just commenced, enable the bees to defend their own by narrowing the entrance, so that only two bees can pass in and out at one time. I have always found this the best remedy; and in several instances I have known those stocks which have been sadly weakened by robbers increase and become most valuable, simply by narrowing the entrance and feeding liberally.

Work for May.

If any month calls for attention in the apiary it is the present one; the practised bee-farmer will keep a constant watch for drones, and if they appear early you may naturally expect early swarms.

> A swarm of bees in May
> Is worth a load of hay.

If the month should unfortunately be wet, or easterly winds prevail, swarming will be kept back.

Queen wasps should be looked for the early part of this month; they are on the wing abundantly in some parts of the country. The late Rev. W. C. Cotton, author of *My Bee-Book*, offered one season to the boys in his large parish school sixpence each for all the queen wasps that were brought to the vicarage during this month; the result was much larger than he expected, and the cost proportionately great, so that he never offered the reward again.

We see with much satisfaction our stocks carrying in a large supply of pollen during this month; this is a good sign of their being in a vigorous condition, and that the hives are filled with brood. If no pollen is brought in, the sooner they are inspected for the cause the better.

Many bee-keepers still cling to the bell-glasses or supers on the top of the hives, and by this means secure sufficient pure honey for their own tables. This prevents swarming, and we believe no system of management which stops the production of swarms can be successful. Still, many persons have confidence in it, and for their sakes we just notice, that if you intend to place supers in the hive it should be done towards the close of the present month. If you have none but straw-hives, cut a round opening at the top of the skep not less than three inches in diameter, over this affix the bell-glass, which should have a small piece of old comb at the top, by way of a guide-comb; the bees will the more readily take to it if the guide-comb is present. *Also*, by all means keep up the temperature in the super, by placing any old clothing over it.

Weak stocks may still require feeding, especially if the month be wet and cold. We have known many stocks to die in May from starvation, but it has been in skep-hives, where their condition was not known; with very slight attention it can scarcely take place when bar-frame hives are used.

Sometimes it may be desirable to drive the bees from a worthless hive to a better receptacle; this should be done now, and the sooner the better.

If any hives show signs of swarming keep a strict watch over them; the bee-farmer's hives throw off swarms very early, *but* the only perceptible signs are clusterings at the entrance for several days. Allow the first swarm to leave, but it is better to prevent any more swarming if you seek for a good honey harvest.

Work for June.

This is the bee-farmer's busy month if a large apiary is under his management and care. He will be kept occupied, hiving swarms, attending to recent swarms in new hives, and in using the honey-extractor.

It has become the fashion in recent years, both in this country and America, to produce artificial swarms. It is generally advised to business-men, who are away from home all day, therefore are unable to look after natural swarming. It may answer and prove successful in some instances, but we confess it has not done so in our apiary. We prefer natural swarming, both for pleasure and profit. Many readers will no doubt consult our pages for several things with which we do not agree; for them we give the best description we have seen of artificial swarming, by Mr. Payne. "The present is a good time for obtaining artificial swarms, and where any form of the bar-hives is used the process is simple, and may be thus effected. From ten to twelve o'clock on a bright morning remove the boards from the top of the parent hive (first puffing a little smoke underneath to make them peaceable), select a bar the comb in which contains both eggs and brood, and if a royal cell all the better, but this is not important; place the bar with comb in some convenient place, so that it is neither bruised nor separated from the bar; then turn up the parent hive, after having fastened down the top, and place the hive intended for the new swarm upon it, observing that the junction is perfect; then by a continuous gentle tapping upon the parent hive for a few minutes a portion of the bees will have ascended into the hive. Remove the parent hive 60 or 100 yards, placing it upon a fresh floor-board, and place the new hive exactly in the place of the old one, and upon the same floor-board; and as quickly as possible introduce the bar of comb, filled with eggs and brood, into its centre; replace the top, and endeavour to have the exterior of the hive as little altered in appearance as possible; it will then be found that the few bees driven into the new hive with the number returning to it that were out at work, with some that may come from the parent hive, will altogether make a fair-sized swarm; the parent hive will, in all probability, give another swarm in about fourteen days."

Those of our readers who are desirous just now to start new colonies in bar-hives may be looking for advice about placing early swarms into them. Always hive the swarm into a straw-skep as being the most convenient for the purpose, as well as being most easily managed. Placing the frame hive on a table convenient or close by the newly hived swarm, and taking off the top board, shake out the swarm from the skep on the bars, and suddenly, before many of them are on the wing, throw a cloth over them for a few minutes until they have gone down beneath the bar-frames, then gently slide the top board over them. We have found the bees take better to these hives when a small quantity of old comb is fastened along the top of the bar; this may readily be effected by means of melted wax run along the bars, and the old comb placed against it before it has time to cool.

If the sun shines full on the hives they should be shaded during the day.

Work for July.

Wherever supers have been used, whether they be bell-glasses or boxes, they must be removed towards the close of this month.

After a wet May it is possible that many late swarms may issue this month; in every case of second and third swarms, let them the same day be returned to the parent hive. It is a very simple matter to return the swarm; after they are hived, if the old or parent hive should happen to be a skep-hive, spread a tablecloth on the ground opposite the stand, remove the old hive and place it on the cloth, supported by a stick about half an inch above the cloth, then knock out the swarm opposite the entrance, they will be received joyfully, and very rarely swarm out a second time, for the cause of it, the young queen, will be speedily carried forth dead.

Hives which are suffered to swarm too often become so weakened that they seldom do much good that season, whilst second and third swarms, more correctly called casts, are useless as separate stocks.

Shading being even more valuable this month than in June, let it not be neglected. In straw hives it is not perhaps so needful as in wood hives; we merely place a white cloth on the top of the hive for two or three hours daily in sultry weather.

In the bee-farmer's hives, each end bar should be inspected at least once each week during the whole of this month. In old stocks in active work good returns of honey may be looked for.

Keep the entrance to the hives clean and allow no obstacle that may in any way prevent free ingress and egress; the prosperity of the colony depends much upon this.

Towards the close of the month, or early in August, your hives may be taken to the heather, if such should be found, about five miles away from their old stand; they will thus glean a second harvest. We have known them to come home with as much as sixty pounds in each hive, and this too after having gathered heavy stores earlier in the season from the clover-fields.

Work for August.

Those of my readers who are well up in the management of their stocks will not need to be told to seek amongst the cottagers in their neighbourhood for condemned stocks. For my part, I have been most successful in the apiaries which are the pride of many of our farmer's wives. In nearly every instance they manage their stocks on the old-fashioned method in small straw skeps, and, if not seen in time, they invariably destroy them over the brimstone-pit. They are, however, very thankful to any one who will save them the trouble of destroying them, or of driving the bees instead. The author of *The Manual of Bee-keeping* states: "Driven-out bees may often be bought in rural districts at about 1s. per pound, and are well worth the money to the advanced apiarian." I have hitherto, by a little courtesy and tact, had no difficulty in securing more condemned stocks than I have been able to find room for just for the trouble of driving them. It would be considered an insult to offer to pay for them in the North of England; they are only too grateful to be saved the trouble, and think this abundant recompense for the bees. Nay, in many instances, I have been asked how much they must pay for my labour in coming to take them. I take with me empty skeps, &c. on an old perambulator, which will hold eight or ten stocks when tied on, returning home just in the cool of the evening.

Every bee-farmer whose stocks are weak should strengthen them with driven stocks, and then feed them up liberally before the winter sets in. Every second swarm or cast should be inspected, for these are often worthless as separate colonies until increased with condemned stocks. Looked at even in this light, driven bees are exceedingly valuable. Many apiarians believe it is impossible to place condemned stocks in empty hives to make them into good colonies. I say, once for all, "try it"; nothing can be done without trying. It is very easy to say it can't be done, but this should never be said without adding, "I will not take the trouble to try." Some of my best and most profitable stocks have been formed solely out of condemned stocks, placed too in empty hives. It is, however, far better if you use the bar-frame hives to build up several bars by tying a little old comb in each bar; this gives them a good start; they lose very little time in fastening the comb to the bars and increasing it by making new comb if they are liberally fed with syrup.

Look carefully over your stocks; if you do not observe them carrying in pollen they should be suspected. If the colony is queenless it will quickly be infested by thieves, and when robbing once commences it is more difficult to stop than many persons imagine. Not only so, the inmates become dispirited, and allow it to become the resort of the bee-moth.

Also, it is well to use every precaution just now, when opening hives or making use of honey, to allow none to lie about; honey being scarce it will cause fighting and much trouble, which can easily be prevented by not giving any occasion for it. Those hives in which the supers still remain had better be attended to. We should now advise all the supers to be at once removed; for, except in favourable localities, very little more honey will be gathered.

Work for September.

About this time complaints are made by practical gardeners of bees eating and destroying their peaches and apricots. It is well known to all careful bee-keepers that their stocks are now, in many instances, in a poor condition; therefore, we do not wonder at their attacking all kinds of ripe and mellow fruits. When the honey-harvest has been plentiful the bees never seek fruits. The best way to keep your bees from thus hurting the gardener is to feed them at this time.

They are now on the alert collecting the last remains

of the honey harvest from the numerous autumnal flowers, chiefly the *Compositæ*, but food is short. Unless they are now liberally fed many stocks will be lost; they should at least be carefully examined, or, what will be best, if you know the actual weight of the hives, weigh them, and, if you believe they do not contain 20 lbs. of honey, they should be fed. Remember! it will be too late to do this in a few weeks, because, when paralysed with cold, they are unable to take in the food if they be ever so willing to do so.

Make the entrance to the hives small, so that not more than three bees can pass and re-pass each other; this advice is needful just now; you have a dreadful enemy to contend against in the shape of wasps, but they are powerless when your stocks are thus aided in their self-defence.

Work for October.

Work begins to be slack, except where the bee-keeper has neglected feeding, which must be done as early in this month as possible, or they will refuse to take in any food. Every hive intended for stocks next year, and which we are expecting to be profitable, should, without any loss of time, be put in a condition for wintering well. First attend well to the ventilation, and especially see that they are well sheltered from the rain, &c. Pan-mugs placed on the top of straw hives as a cover or screen from the weather may do for rough, unthinking bee-owners, but should never be adopted by those who love their bees; on the contrary, make good straw covers, or, if you can afford it, wood covers, which are the best. Break up weak stocks, and unite them with a stronger colony. In straw hives it is well to make a small hole through the centre of every comb, to enable the bees to pass in any direction with comfort, and without having to traverse round the edge of every comb when the thermometer is below zero.

Guard against the entrance of the small field or harvest mouse; where your stocks are seated on low stands a strong temptation is held out to them of snug winter quarters: make the entrance small, then they are easily kept out. I have known hives completely ruined by this enemy, who is certainly not dormant in the bee-hive, whatever he may be in the cornfield.

Work for November.

If you suspect any stocks have not sufficient food in the hive for their winter consumption, the sooner it is given the better.

In making the entrance small allow sufficient room to promote a thorough ventilation. If the hive is under shelter, so as to exclude rain or moisture in any form, then leave out the feeding-plug all the winter; we need not fear cold air or frost; a far worse enemy is damp, which will cause dysentery, and decay of the combs.

Some bee-farmers wrap a layer of hay-bands round all their hives during the winter months, which is doubtless beneficial, especially if a good ventilation be maintained. Straw hives do not require much attention in this respect.

If you desire to remove your apiary to a more convenient place it should be done now. Much has been written about the hives with the entrance facing towards the north; mine have generally been towards the sunrising (east), thus receiving the benefit of his early beams. I cannot state how a northern aspect may suit them, having no experience, but I still hold the opinion that bees do far better if kept on single pedestals or stands.

Bee-houses cannot be too strongly condemned; they are only a harbouring-place for vermin, and cause the death of many a valuable queen by causing her to mistake the entrance upon returning to the hive after her wedding flight.

WORK FOR DECEMBER.

It is generally supposed that this is the holiday season of the bee-farmer, for in this month of all others he cannot have much to do in his apiary.

If he can spare a holiday to visit his neighbours far or near who keep bees, it may be well spent in comparing notes about the management of their stocks. We fear it will be found the majority of bee-keepers are still wedded to the old straw-skep, followed by the brimstone pit in the autumn. If we can, however, enlighten their minds by showing them a better way, especially by holding out to their view a few golden coins as a result of their labours, it may help to make them excellent bee-farmers. It will be impossible to overstock this land of plenty, and why should we be compelled to go abroad for our chief supply of honey? The market never seems to be overstocked with this commodity, and as good samples of honey may be found in English apiaries as ever came from the Continent, if not superior.

Let us try to raise British bee-farming to the rank of a science and we need not fear any other country in the world outstripping us in the race.

THE END.

BIBLIOLIFE

Old Books Deserve a New Life
www.bibliolife.com

Did you know that you can get most of our titles in our trademark **EasyScript**™ print format? **EasyScript**™ provides readers with a larger than average typeface, for a reading experience that's easier on the eyes.

Did you know that we have an ever-growing collection of books in many languages?

Order online:
www.bibliolife.com/store

Or to exclusively browse our **EasyScript**™ collection:
www.bibliogrande.com

At BiblioLife, we aim to make knowledge more accessible by making thousands of titles available to you – quickly and affordably.

Contact us:
BiblioLife
PO Box 21206
Charleston, SC 29413